"Take Courage,
I Have Overcome the World."

MINUTE MEDITATIONS FOR EACH DAY

By
REV. BEDE NAEGELE, O.C.D.

Illustrated

CATHOLIC BOOK PUBLISHING CO.
New York

CONTENTS

NIHIL OBSTAT: Daniel V. Flynn, J.C.D.
Censor Librorum

IMPRIMATUR: Joseph T. O'Keefe
Vicar General, Archdiocese of New York

(T-190)

PREFACE

SMALL in size but rich in content, that is an apt description of *Minute Meditations for Each Day*.

A thought for each day of the year is drawn from Sacred Scripture, requiring little commentary, but reflection and prayer.

The soul that every day will meditate upon these thoughts—which in the light of Revelation are directly addressed to our will—will very soon acquire the sense of God's presence.

Every thought will be like a spark that rises from the flames of Divine love, because the soul will continue this intimate conversation, according to grace and personal desires.

There is nothing difficult or abstract in this little book, nor is there anything new or intricate—just the traditional doctrine with its unique strength.

This book is for everybody: for the devout and the person on the street alike, without distinction. The author has not addressed himself to any age, class, or spiritual condition in particular; he only wishes to serve the truth because his work is for all people, as meditation should be.

If today is not the time for words because what is important is action, then it is also the time to meditate, especially for us who live in the midst of a civilization that has the painful privilege of hindering human beings in their right to find themselves! Still more to find their God. In our times, the words of Jeremiah are most appropriate: "The world is in a state of desolation because no one takes it to heart" (Jeremiah 12:11).

Pope Pius XII said: "It is necessary to renew everything from its very foundation!" A purpose that should be imprinted upon every heart. But this foundation is none other than our approach to Jesus Christ and His Word as we find it in the pages of the Gospel. What matters is not to discover the deep secrets of the universe, but to understand this simple truth: "That which is not eternal is nothing." This is Jesus Christ Who, therefore, is the sole Reality.

But in order to comprehend this we must meditate and pray, according to Jesus' admonition: "Be alert and pray!" These words were not spoken only for His time but for all times, unto eternity.

If anyone would serve me, let him follow me. —Jn 12:26

JAN. 1

REFLECTION. Let this be my goal for this year: to follow Jesus through all the paths that He may lead me—no matter how difficult or painful they may be.

What is there to fear if the Master is with me and He Himself opens the way for me? In faith, I know that this path leads me to the Father and always ends in victory and glory.

PRAYER. *O Lord, take me by the hand and lead me to my blessed goal: to possess You for all eternity*

If anyone is in Christ he is a new creation. —2 Cor 5:17

JAN. 2

REFLECTION. If I have become a new creation, the old self of sin can no longer rule in me. My whole life—thoughts, words, actions, and sufferings—must bear the Divine stamp.

Today, I want to dedicate myself uniquely to this point.

PRAYER. *O Lord, grant me each day a new fervor, fresh energy, and a more selfless love. Root out whatever in me is not from You, so that You can grow ever more in me.*

JAN.
3

Cast all your cares on him because he cares for you. —1 Pt 5:7

REFLECTION.   God directs all things. It is useless for me to become alarmed, and give way
to haste and anxiety which only make me
forget God!

I do not want to neglect anything of what I
must do myself, but I also want to entrust to
God all that He alone can do. He takes care of
me.

PRAYER.   *My Lord and Father, free me from
all base earthly cares. Amidst the disquiet of
this world help me to find my rest in You.*

JAN.
4

Your attitude must be that of
Christ.   —Phil 2:5

REFLECTION.   If my attitude were that of
Christ, my life and my activity would be pur-
ified of all that is incomplete, careless,
worldly, and self-centered.

To be a Christian involves a commitment. I
want to conform my day according to the
Model Who is Christ, so that it may be spiritually fruitful for eternity.

PRAYER.   *My Savior, inspire me with Your attitude, and make me avoid all that is opposed
to You. Let my life be as straight as the path
that leads to the Father.*

8

The Teacher is here, asking for you. —Jn 11:28

JAN. 5

REFLECTION. God calls me through the medium of my duty. But He also calls me through the events of every day and every hour—the interruptions and contradictions He sends. Am I always aware of this?

There is only one response to this Divine call. It is a courageous and faithful "I am ready."

PRAYER. *Heavenly Father, help me to hear Your call in all that happens to me. Let me fulfill Your will with patience and joy.*

Rise up in splendor! Your light has come, the glory of the Lord shines upon you. —Is 60:1

JAN. 6

REFLECTION. Christ reveals His glory. Therefore I too must try to be a manifestation of God. I must be a living testimony to His glory, always trying to deepen my spiritual life—according to Christ's spirit and will—in poverty, humility, and love for God and others.

Can I say that I am an "epiphany," that is, God's manifestation? What do I lack in this regard?

PRAYER. *My Lord and my God, grant me the grace to mirror Your own image! Make me see You in everything, that I may honor and love You in all persons.*

JAN.
7

God who is mighty has done great things for me, holy is his name.

—Lk 1:49

REFLECTION. Every passing day tells me that I am a child of grace: God's benefits are innumerable in my daily life.

This is why I wish to give Him thanks through my dedication and fidelity until I die.

PRAYER. *Lord, do not let me refuse your mercy. Forgive my abuses of Your grace. In the future be merciful and lenient toward me.*

JAN.
8

The apostles left everything, and became his followers. —Jn 5:11

REFLECTION. To abandon everything and follow Christ! Am I ready to do this?

Or is there something in my life that I cling to and am unwilling to sacrifice, even if God wishes it?

PRAYER. *Dear Lord, You are my everything. Make me love You above all in this world. Grant that I may leave everything to find You.*

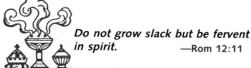

Do not grow slack but be fervent in spirit.
—Rom 12:11

JAN. 9

REFLECTION. O how often I defraud God in the small events of daily life. Sometimes I do so by my lack of fervor, and at other times by aspiring to great things and grand actions for my own pride.

Yet God does not look upon "how much" but rather on the "how"; therefore a small thing becomes great if it is done with much love.

PRAYER. *Heavenly Father, grant that I may be zealous and faithful in small things. Let all my days give glory to You and bring Your blessings upon me.*

But the Lord keeps faithful; he it is who will strengthen you and guard you against the evil one.
—2 Thes 3:3

JAN. 10

REFLECTION. God's faithfulness should be my comfort and my encouragement when I feel weary and disheartened in performing my duties.

My Father never abandons me. He helps me according to the measure of my faith.

PRAYER. *Faithful God, strengthen my faith. Make, me willing and obedient in fulfilling Your will, even when this is difficult for me.*

JAN. 11

No more than a branch can bear fruit of itself apart from the vine, can you bear fruit apart from me.
—Jn 15:4

REFLECTION. Without Christ and His grace all our efforts and actions are in vain. With Christ and His grace everything, even the most insignificant act of our daily lives, becomes fruitful for all eternity.

My crop will be plentiful only if I abandon myself to His will and live the life of grace.

PRAYER. *My Savior, instill Your Divine grace in me. Let everything I think, or say, or do, even my most mundane actions, show forth Your grace acting in me.*

JAN. 12

Then you will lead a life worthy of the Lord.
—Col 1:10

REFLECTION. In my daily living I am necessarily occupied with ordinary and secular things. But I wish to sanctify everything I do through supernatural intentions.

In this way, my life will be pleasing to God and enable me to reach Him.

PRAYER. *Father, grant that my life may be a sacred service to You. May I always bring honor to You, and draw down Your blessings upon me.*

My grace is enough for you.
—2 Cor 12:9

JAN.
13

REFLECTION. How often in my life I have been deluded and deceived because I have trusted exclusively in myself or in others! Why don't I turn directly to God?

He is Omnipotent. With His grace I will become invincible, even though the powers of hell rage against me.

PRAYER. *Most holy and almighty God, help me to turn to You in every need and danger. Arm me with Your strength, so that I may overcome all difficulties.*

Those that sow in tears shall reap rejoicing.
—Ps 126:5

JAN.
14

REFLECTION. How would I be able to endure this earthly life, heavy and burdensome as it is, if I did not know that it is just an instant compared with eternity! Now is the time to sow, and after a short interval the harvest will be gathered.

Through patient endurance of the sufferings of this life the eternal glory will be attained.

PRAYER. *God of love, do not abandon me in the midst of darkness. Grant that my troubles and needs may enrich my soul and bring it safely to eternal life with You.*

JAN. 15 *You are the salt of the earth.*
—Mt 5:13

REFLECTION. I am not alone in the world. Rather I have been born into a large community of souls to whom I have obligations, not only as a human being but as a child of God.

Do I realize that I can be an influence for good but also for evil in the world, and that on the day of the last judgment God will not only judge my own soul, but also the souls of my neighbors?

PRAYER. *My Lord and my God, grant that I may bring You to all people by the way I live my life. Help me to do my share in changing the world for the better.*

JAN. 16 *If we love one another God dwells in us, and his love is brought to perfection in us.* ——Jn 4:12

REFLECTION. I possess God by loving Him above all and everyone else for His sake, for God is love and this is His just command.

Therefore, I want to meet all human beings with love, without exception, and then God will dwell in my heart.

PRAYER. *My Father, give me the spirit of love, and grant that I may see You in all human beings.*

14

Whoever does not accept the reign of God like a little child, shall not take part in it. —Mk 10:15

JAN. 17

REFLECTION. How little God demands of us in order to enter into His kingdom: ingenuity, fidelity, and a child's humility! Yet He demands much prayer and effort to overcome human pride.

The Kingdom of God cannot be bought, cannot be obtained by human force, cannot be seized by cunning. It is given as a gift to those who have a childlike spirit.

PRAYER. *Good Father, I give you thanks because I can call myself Your child and an heir to Your Kingdom. Give me the innocence of a child, that I may be sure of Your fatherly love.*

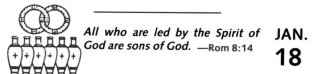

All who are led by the Spirit of God are sons of God. —Rom 8:14

JAN. 18

REFLECTION. Are my actions motivated by worldly gratifications and advantages, or by God's will?

My whole life should breathe Divine things, because being a child of God is at the same time both a gift and a duty.

PRAYER. *Heavenly Father, fill me with Your Spirit. Grant that I may be Your obedient instrument at every moment of my life.*

JAN. 19

Venerate the Lord, that is, Christ, in your hearts. —1 Pt 3:15

REFLECTION. If I believe in God's presence within me I will not permit anything profane or unworthy of Him in me. I will avoid everything that is not in accordance with His will because He is all-Holy.

My only fear must be to displease Him, and my only concern to give all worship and honor to Him Who is my Lord.

PRAYER. *Holy Spirit, come and fill me with Your grace. Grant that Your Kingdom will come in me, and through me will also come to all others.*

JAN. 20

For God has shone in our hearts, that we in turn might make known the glory of God. —2 Cor 4:6

REFLECTION. My mission in the world is to be a light in the darkness and a guide to others in their journey through life.

Therefore I must strive, with God's help, to receive His grace, and so to bring Him to all persons who are in need of Him.

PRAYER. *Good Shepherd. grant that I may always be Your helper. Let me serve You with absolute faithfulness.*

Each one of you is a son of God because of your faith in Christ Jesus.
—Gal 3:26

JAN. 21

REFLECTION. As children of God, we must give ourselves in love, one to another. We must help each other in our troubles, as is proper for brothers and sisters.

Do I think of all human beings as my brothers and sisters, and that I have duties and responsibilities toward them?

PRAYER. *Jesus, my brother, grant that I may love all human beings as You love them, even to the point of giving myself up for them by total self-denial.*

Whoever does the will of my heavenly Father, is brother and sister and mother to me.
—Mt 12:50

JAN. 22

REFLECTION. When God's will speaks everything else must remain silent. Even the greatest creature must humble himself. Above the ties of blood there exists the community of those who have done the will of God.

Christ belongs to them and they belong to Him, in the same way as brothers and sisters and mother belong one to the other.

PRAYER. *Lord, grant that I may do your will and not mine, always and above all.*

JAN. 23

Do not conform yourselves to this age. —Rom 12:2

REFLECTION. My goal is to become more and more like God. This requires a change of my inner self. I now need that renewal of mind and heart which will free me from the spirit of the world and make me adhere to Christ, through the working of the Holy Spirit.

I must examine myself to see where I stand in this and pray for grace to change what needs to be changed.

PRAYER. *Merciful God, deliver me from a worldly spirit, that I may serve You alone with a pure heart. Enlighten me by the power of the Holy Spirit to conform myself to You.*

JAN. 24

With age-old love I have loved you; so I have kept my mercy toward you. —Jer 31:3

REFLECTION. God is essentially love. Therefore, everything He commands me to do is because He loves me whether it brings me joy or pain.

I must never forget this, especially in times of difficulty and trial.

PRAYER. *Beloved Father, grant me the assurance of Your love. Then even at the hour of my Gethsemani I shall never cease to have peace in my heart.*

I myself am the bread of life. No one who comes to me shall ever be hungry. —Jn 6:35

JAN. 25

REFLECTION. Bread gives life and energy; but it must be eaten. Therefore, our Savior, as Bread for the soul, wishes to be received and eaten with the right disposition of sorrow for sin, humility, and thankfulness for His great gift to us.

Worship and admiration are not enough to save the soul from death of starvation. Why don't I approach the Sacred banquet more often?

PRAYER. *My faithful Lord and Savior, be the food of my soul now and forever.*

If anyone comes to me without turning his back on his father and mother, his wife and children, his brothers and sisters, indeed his very self, he cannot be my follower. —Lk 25:26

JAN. 26

REFLECTION. The Savior wants allies not sympathizers. I must renounce even my dearest loved ones if they hinder me from following Christ.

Am I ready to make any sacrifice, without exceptions, for the cause of Christ?

PRAYER. *My Jesus, grant that I may be able to renounce everything, even to the most cherished things, so that I may be with You.*

JAN. 27

Do not be conquered by evil, but conquer evil with good.

—Rom 12:21

REFLECTION. Evil has a creative force. If I pay back evil with evil, I do not conquer it, but rather I am conquered by it and become its ally.

If, instead, I oppose good to evil, I destroy the roots of evil in me with the help of God's grace, and I do much good. Why don't I always act thus?

PRAYER. *Lord, victory is always on Your side. Strengthen me that I may conquer evil.*

JAN. 28

Be imitators of God as his dear children, follow the way of love.

—Eph 5:1

REFLECTION. The life of Christ was full of love, sacrifice and self-denial up to His Death. I am called to follow His example of love.

This means not to live for myself but for Him, Who loved me first, and for those in whom He wants to be loved.

PRAYER. *My Lord and my Savior, because You loved me You gave up everything for me. Grant me the grace to repay Your love with love, and Your fidelity with fidelity.*

Take heed, therefore, how you hear. —Lk 8:18

REFLECTION. God speaks to me in many different ways: through the Scriptures, through the circumstances of my life, with its joys and sufferings, and through the people I meet.

Do I always listen to and obey His voice? What a terrible thing it would be if God did not speak to me anymore because I do not listen to Him!

PRAYER. *Speak to me, Lord; Your servant is listening.*

Like a weaned child on its mother's lap, so is my soul within me. —Ps 131:4

REFLECTION. Ambition and selfishness make us demanding, uneasy, and unhappy. The more I try to correspond to everything that God gives me and to renounce those things that He denies me, the more peacefully and happily I shall rest in Him.

I shall try to trust in God like a contented child lying in its mother's arms.

PRAYER. *Lord, grant me a genuine love for You and Your grace; then I shall be rich enough and shall not seek anything else.*

JAN.
31

You are not of the world.
—Mt 5:14

REFLECTION. How can I in my surroundings be a light that will illuminate the dark lowliness of daily life; a light that warms, enlightens and vivifies?

I can do so only if I myself am in the luminous circle of God. Christ must enlighten me. Then I will be able to radiate His light widely and effectively to others.

PRAYER. *My Lord and my God, You are my light and my strength. Grant that Your light will never cease to shine in me.*

FEB.
1

Everyone who grows angry with his brother shall be liable to judgment.
—Mt 5:22

REFLECTION. A wicked thought destroys the foundation of human society and uproots mutual trust and love.

Hence, Christ demands a perfect and fraternal kindness that will not tolerate even a bad thought about one's neighbor, for external courtesy and politeness are not enough. What is my attitude toward my neighbor?

PRAYER. *God of love, grant that my heart may be enlarged and my love enriched. Let me always be worthy of Your love.*

And the world with its seductions is passing away, but the man who does God's will endures forever.
—1 Jn 2:17

FEB. 2

REFLECTION. I am also part of the world, subject to its temporal law. But God's love has called me to eternity. I live, to be renewed; I die, to live forever.

It depends upon my faithful fulfillment of God's will whether my life will be one of everlasting joy. Am I faithfully fulfilling His will?

PRAYER. *Heavenly Father, make me always walk in Your life. Grant that one day I may return to Your everlasting bliss.*

For here we have no lasting city; we are seeking one which is to come.
—Heb 13:14

FEB. 3

REFLECTION. Faith in eternity does not seek to escape from the world, but rather to conquer it. Let's not proclaim ourselves as incompetent but as sacred. Let's attend to our daily tasks with courage and joy, always carrying our eternal goal in our hearts so that we may not be lacking in perseverance.

This should be our daily task. Do I measure up to this?

PRAYER. *My Lord and my God, give me a deep yearning for You, so that the world may not enslave me.*

23

FEB. 4

Come by yourselves to an out-of-the-way place and rest a little.
—Mk 6:31

REFLECTION. Our inner life needs the best; it needs solitude. Indeed, the soul needs times of silence that it may not be overcome by dissipation. In this way it can be recollected in God and be prepared for all the tasks and struggles that lie ahead.

During this time of meditation we communicate with God and learn what He expects of us. Do I regularly seek this solitude?

PRAYER. *Lord, calm my soul so that I may silently listen to and treasure Your word.*

FEB. 5

For when I am powerless, it is then that I am strong.
—2 Cor 12:10

REFLECTION. Of themselves, human beings are nothing, but with God's grace, they are everything.

God bestows His grace upon all who acknowledge their own weakness and pray with humility and confidence.

PRAYER. *Eternal God, let me recognize the riches of Your grace. May I be forever grateful to You and worthy to receive additional grace to deepen my spiritual life.*

You will live in my love if you keep my commandments.

—Jn 15:10

FEB.
6

REFLECTION. God desires obedient children who show their love through the faithful fulfillment of their duties.

Love is not only an emotion but an action, a living action. Is this true of my love?

PRAYER. *Merciful Father, save me from indifference and mere external worship. Let me always try to follow in the way of Your commandments with ever greater fidelity.*

God is love.

—Jn 4:16

FEB.
7

REFLECTION. God is love. Thus, everything that God does or permits is the consequence of His love.

What a pity that this love is frequently unknown or misunderstood!

PRAYER. *Ineffable Lord, make me think of You unselfishly. Let me discover Your love in everything, so that my life may truly be happy and blessed.*

25

FEB. 8

While we live we are constantly being delivered to death for Jesus' sake. —2 Cor 4:10

REFLECTION. We are not like Christ if we do not share in His sufferings. His Passion must become my passion.

This is how I show forth His life within me.

PRAYER. *Savior of the world, be my guide in all my ways. Help me, so that at difficult times I may remain faithful to You.*

FEB. 9

Power went out from him which cured all. —Lk 6:19

REFLECTION. Christ wishes to reveal Himself as powerful in our weakness. He waits only for us to reach out to Him with unshakable faith.

Even today His power is manifest. Why don't I try to reach out to Him?

PRAYER. *Omnipotent Father, strengthen my faith and my trust. Grant me all the graces that I need.*

26

John was clothed in camel's hair, and wore a leather belt around his waist. —Mk 1:6

FEB. 10

REFLECTION. How completely different is Christ from John His precursor! His piety is natural and life-endorsing. His message is a message of joy. There is nothing gloomy about Him; everything is bathed in light and love.

What is my attitude toward the things of this world? Why do I think that I must become unnatural and opposed to life in order to be religious?

PRAYER. *My Savior, I thank You also for the goods of this world. Grant that they may become a blessing for me.*

Whenever you pray, go to your room, close the door, and pray to your Father in private. —Mt 6:6

FEB. 11

REFLECTION. To pray in our room means to immerse ourselves interiorly and exteriorly in silence and recollection. This in no way excludes a joyful profession of faith.

Christ prayed frequently enough in public and with a loud voice. Would I have the courage to do the same?

PRAYER. *God of holiness, fill me with holy fear in Your presence. Teach me how to pray to You.*

FEB. 12

This kind does not leave but by prayer and fasting. —Mt 17:21

REFLECTION. Prayer by itself is not enough. It must be made fruitful by fasting.

This means by sacrifice, by the denial of our own desires, comforts, and search for pleasure. Then miracles can be accomplished.

PRAYER. *Eternal God, Your grace is my hope and my strength. Grant me a heart joyfully willing to sacrifice, so that I may be worthy of Your help.*

FEB. 13

The sabbath was made for man, not man for the sabbath. —Mk 2:27

REFLECTION. Letter-perfect submission paralyzes and kills. God's commandments are intended to strengthen and encourage the life of the soul, not to suffocate it.

The stamp of Christ is love. When this is lacking, the mere observance of the law accomplishes nothing.

PRAYER. *Heavenly Father, sanctify my heart and fill it with the Spirit of Your love. Grant that I may grow from day to day in this Holy Spirit.*

You too go along to my vineyard.
—Mt 20:4

REFLECTION.   God's vineyard is not only inside the soul but also outside. It is in the world that we manifest His grace in our soul by doing everything for the sake of His love.

In this way my ordinary deeds become work in the Lord's vineyard. Do I think about this every day?

PRAYER.   *My Lord, I give You my entire life. May everything that I think, say, do, or suffer be consecrated to You and be blessed by You.*

The man who loves his life loses it, while the man who hates his life in this world preserves it to life eternal.   —Jn 12:25

REFLECTION.   Natural life is the foundation of spiritual life; but it cannot become an end in itself because it bears within it the seed of death.

The spiritual life is active only where there is sacrifice for the sake of God's love.

PRAYER.   *God of holiness, make me faithful and strong. Willingly I will sacrifice everything that is not pleasing to You, so that one day I may obtain life in You.*

FEB.
16

The way we know we remain in him and he in us is that he has given us of his Spirit. —1 Jn 4:13

REFLECTION. God in me and I in Him. This means that I must not let myself be dominated by my natural instincts, but must allow the Holy Spirit to be the driving force of my life.

Is this true in me?

PRAYER. *Eternal God, pour forth Your Spirit into my heart. Let me go through this life as a pilgrim heaven bound.*

———————

FEB.
17

I am the way.   —Jn 14:6

REFLECTION. As the sea is necessary to the ships that sail on it, so Christ is needed by our souls. He is the Way.

Those who are not in Christ but go their own way will never attain their goal.

PRAYER. *My Savior, be always at my side and lead me, through this life on earth, to Your eternal dwelling, to Your Father and mine.*

Treat others the way you would have them treat you. —Mt 7:12

FEB. 18

REFLECTION. Refraining from evil is not enough. God commands us to do good.

Is this the rule of my life? One day I will be judged according to the deeds of love.

PRAYER. *Loving Savior, pour Your love into my heart. Make me ready and willing to give myself to others as You have given Yourself for me.*

That we have passed from death to life we know because we love the brothers. —1 Jn 3:14

FEB. 19

REFLECTION. Love for neighbor is the sign of new life in God. Those who bear God within them and love Him will also extend their love to their neighbor.

Those who show no concern for their neighbor show that they have not found the life in God, or that they have lost it again.

PRAYER. *Father of all creatures, give me a child's heart. Make me reach out to my brothers and sisters with love and compassion.*

31

FEB. 20

In giving alms you are not to let your left hand know what your right hand is doing. —Mt 6:3

REFLECTION. To seek human gratitude and acknowledgment is to seek not God's glory but to satisfy our own selfish pride.

Those who wish to please God must do good for His sake. Hence, every offering bears the mark of a true and unconditional dedication.

PRAYER. *Lord, grant me a pure love that neither knows nor wishes anything else than to give You honor and glory.*

FEB. 21

When you pray do not behave like the hypocrites. —Mt 6:5

REFLECTION. Deceit and hypocrisy are poison to the soul. Nothing is hidden from God and He knows what we really are.

Can we attempt to be what we are not? God is not deceived by our pretenses.

PRAYER. *Eternal light, kindly enlighten my spirit. Let me always walk in truth and humility before You.*

I thought I had toiled in vain, and for nothing. —Is 49:4

FEB.
22

REFLECTION. God does not know the words "in vain."

Whatever is done for the love of God remains and bears fruit for all eternity, even if it goes unrecognized in this world.

PRAYER. *Loving Father, do not look upon what I have done but upon what I aspired to do. Let Your blessings descend upon me and grant that, one day, my good will may share in the glory You have prepared for those who do Your will.*

You too are living stones, built as an edifice of the spirit. —1 Pt 2:5

FEB.
23

REFLECTION. To be stones used in the building up of God's temple! What an honor and distinction But I must let myself be chiseled and molded by God. Otherwise I will be rejected by Him as a useless stone.

Am I always aware of this obligation?

PRAYER. *My Father, I give You thanks because You take care of me. May Your will be accomplished in me.*

FEB. 24

Say, 'Yes' when you mean 'Yes' and 'No' when you mean 'No.'
—Mt 5:37

REFLECTION. Honesty must be complete; otherwise it is dishonesty. Only by perfect, unconditional honesty can people's confidence be won, not by affirmations and oaths.

The confidence that is lost by dishonesty cannot be regained by a superabundance of affirmations.

PRAYER. *God of truth, grant that everything I say or do may come from a contrite and upright heart, so that one day I may be worthy to stand before You.*

———————

FEB. 25

My hour has not yet come.
—Jn 2:4

REFLECTION. The "Hour of God" unites us with God and frees us from human beings. God does not fall short. When His Hour comes, He intervenes.

Hence, we need more patience and trust in His holy will and in His Divine Providence.

PRAYER. *Heavenly Father, let me place everything in Your hands. Guide me in the way of my life and make me obey Your Divine will with firm faith.*

Jesus made no answer.

—Lk 23:9

FEB.
26

REFLECTION. Jesus never forces our will or our love. He remains silent when we renounce Him by sin or by our lack of response to the graces He sends us.

When we feel He is far away, we should examine our attitude toward Him.

PRAYER. *My Savior, stay near me. Make me always hear Your voice and do everything You say to me.*

When a person strikes you on the right cheek, turn and offer him the other.

—Mt 5:39

FEB.
27

REFLECTION. Persons possessed by evil do not improve when evil is paid back with another evil. They are conquered only by goodness.

To bear wrongs in patience is the real meaning of love and only this has redeeming value. Am I prepared for such love?

PRAYER. *Eternal God, help me to suffer for others that I may obtain Your blessings for them and myself.*

FEB. 28
Such obedience is the will of God. . . . Live as free men, but do not use your freedom as a cloak for vice.
—1 Pt 2:16

REFLECTION. Human beings are free but remain forever subject to God. Thus freedom is protected against the abuses that produce evil.

Do I feel fully responsible for everything I do or neglect to do?

PRAYER. *Omnipotent Father, make me faithful to all my duties. Show me Your will and let it be my sole rule of conduct.*

MAR. 1
If a man wishes to come after me, he must deny his very self.
—Mt 16:24

REFLECTION. The struggle against self is not an easy one and requires constant effort. Its purpose is to rid ourselves of all that separates us from the will of God.

But the reward is great and with God's grace and our own effort we become better persons—disciples of Christ.

PRAYER. *My Lord and my Savior, it is a grace to follow You. Grant me steadfastness and a spirit of sacrifice so that through difficult times I will not forget my glorious end.*

My heart is broken with sorrow.
—Mt 26:38

MAR.
2

REFLECTION. The Savior was at the end of His strength, afflicted and exhausted to death. But He surrendered Himself to His Father's will and the Father comforted Him.

I will think of this at the hour of my Gethsemani when I find no one to comfort me.

PRAYER. *Heavenly Father, be always near me and strengthen me, Your child, as You did Your Divine Son. Let Your holy will be fulfilled in me and through me.*

Am I not to drink the cup the Father has given me? —Jn 18:11

MAR.
3

REFLECTION. The cup of the Father comes from the hands of the Father. This is why our Savior drinks it, knowing that it contains the sins of the whole world.

Why do I hesitate to drink my cup? Don't I realize that it is part of God's saving plan?

PRAYER. *My Father, I trust in You. Strengthen my weakness and make me always more generous in the spirit of sacrifice.*

MAR. 4

Those who belong to Christ Jesus have crucified their flesh with its passions and desires. —Gal 5:24

REFLECTION. It is a manifest contradiction and indeed impossible to wish to belong to the innocent Christ and, at the same time, still live in sin.

A life of union with Christ demands a daily crucifixion of the flesh, absolute denial of everything that separates us from Him.

PRAYER. *Lamb of God, take my heart with all its weaknesses and errors. Make me abhor sin and serve You all my life with loving dedication.*

MAR. 5

The way we came to understand love was that he laid down his life for us. —1 Jn 3:16

REFLECTION. God has loved us even to death on the Cross—unto folly as St. Paul tells us. Never can we doubt God's love for us.

Anything coming from His hands is love, nothing else but love, Divine love.

PRAYER. *Most loving Redeemer, I give You thanks because You love me so much that You have died for me. Grant that I may love You back in the same manner.*

We too must lay down our lives for our brothers. —1 Jn 3:16

MAR. 6

REFLECTION. To love means to give our most prized possession, our very selves, our own lives. Am I ready to do this?

Is my life faithful to the words: "One for all"? Only in this way can I be Christ-like and worthy of Christ.

PRAYER. *O my Savior, Your entire life was a loving immolation. Let my own life be filled with deeds of love, so that I may become like You.*

My Father, if it is possible, let this cup pass me by. Still, let it be as you would have it, not as I.
—Mt 26:39

MAR. 7

REFLECTION. My Father, if it is possible. . . . But this was not possible for the Redemption.

In like manner, God cannot take every cup away from me, because this is necessary for my salvation.

PRAYER. *Father, I know that it is not the human will but only Your will which is our Paradise. May Your will alone be done also in me.*

MAR. 8

This day you will be with me in paradise. —Lk 23:43

REFLECTION. This is God's answer to the supplicating cry of the repentant thief.

God does not reject anyone who even at the last minute raises a longing and repentant heart to Him.

PRAYER. *Heavenly Father, I come before You like the prodigal son. Be merciful and lenient to me, especially in the hour of my death.*

MAR. 9

Did not the Messiah have to undergo all this so as to enter into his glory? —Lk 24:26

REFLECTION. Every sorrowful way is a Divine way that can lead me to eternal happiness.

Therefore, I want to follow it strengthened by keeping my eyes on Him Who goes before me and helps me carry my cross.

PRAYER. *God of love, the Cross is to me the key to paradise. Let me never forget this so that I will never reject it.*

The stone which the builders rejected has become the cornerstone. —Ps 117:22

MAR
10

REFLECTION. Rejected by human beings on Good Friday, acknowledged by God on Easter Sunday and made the cornerstone—Christ takes His place in the center of history.

Those who place their foundations in Him and His Church will never be lost. However, those who reject Him will themselves be rejected.

PRAYER. *Christ, my King, I promise to be obedient and faithful to You until death.*

The power that has conquered the world is this faith of ours.
—1 Jn 5:4

MAR.
11

REFLECTION. Faith has a conquering power over the world. It joins us to the Conqueror of the world, risen from the grave.

The more solid my faith is in Christ Jesus, our Lord, the better I will triumph over the world with its sorrows and its joys.

PRAYER. *Heavenly Father, grant me a living faith that I may discover eternal things behind those that are merely human, and may happily arrive at my everlasting dwelling.*

41

MAR. 12

You will suffer in the world. But take courage! I have overcome the world.
—Jn 16:33

SALVS

REFLECTION. The essence of the world is human exaltation of self. Christ overcame this by His obedience.

We too will overcome it if first we conquer our own base, selfish nature and totally abandon ourselves to God. Am I ready to do this?

PRAYER. *Lord, let me die to the world so that I may live only for You.*

MAR. 13

'Peace' is my farewell to you, my peace is my gift to you.
—Jn 14:27

REFLECTION. Christ has associated peace with His person. Far from him and deprived of Him, the world will be eternally without peace.

Happy are those who welcome Him and take refuge in His peace. Am I among this group?

PRAYER. *God of peace, put an end to worldly strife and grant us Your peace.*

If we have died with Christ, we believe that we are also to live with him. —Rom 6:8

MAR. 14

REFLECTION. Through struggle, victory; through darkness, light; through death, life.

This has been promised to all those who persevere to the end in the way of the Cross in this earthly life.

PRAYER. *My Father, give me patience in all my afflictions. Grant that under the weight of the Cross I may never forget the blessing of the Cross.*

I give them eternal life, and they shall never perish. No one shall snatch them out of my hand. —Jn 10:28

MAR. 15

REFLECTION. Christians may fall, but so long as they clasp the merciful hand of the Good Shepherd they will never perish.

Stronger than all the faults and defects of human beings are God's eternal love and fidelity.

PRAYER. *My God, truly infinite are Your goodness and mercy. Accept, then, the "thanksgiving" of my life; let my heart be always pure and holy, so that You may dwell therein.*

43

MAR. 16

My thoughts are not your thoughts, nor are your ways my ways. —Is 55:8

REFLECTION. Whoever does not think the thoughts of God will never walk in God's ways either. Other ways presuppose other thoughts.

Think always of those things that are God's and then your ways will be the ways of God.

PRAYER. *Lord, deliver me from selfishness. In all my ways, let Your will be my guiding star.*

MAR. 17

It is much better for you that I go. —Jn 16:7

REFLECTION. Christ's return to the Father served to make the disciples mature in faith. Their hopes were not destroyed but fulfilled.

Thus, God often takes something from us—but only to give us something better. He destroys and breaks so that upon the earthly ruins the temple of the Holy Spirit may be erected.

PRAYER. *Lord, do what You will: You know all things. I trust in You completely.*

And know that I am with you always, until the end of the world.
—Mt 28:20

MAR. 18

REFLECTION. He will be with us "always"—hence, even today in every need of soul or body He is there.

He is never deceived or impatient but always ready and willing to help. What then can I still fear?

PRAYER. *Merciful Savior, You want to be my companion in life. Make me stay ever close to You, even when You lead me on the way of the Cross.*

Joseph her husband was an upright man.
—Mt 1:19

MAR. 19

REFLECTION. With these words Sacred Scripture pays the highest compliment to St. Joseph. He was an upright man, one who fulfilled his duties to God, to his neighbor, and to himself in a perfect manner.

By faithfulness to God's will in all doubts and trials—not by extraordinary things—he merited to be the foster-father of the Son of God, and the husband of His Virgin Mother.

PRAYER. *St. Joseph, let me follow you by doing my duties with full dedication and faithfulness, that I too may earn God's favor.*

45

MAR. 20

As generous distributors of God's manifold grace, put your gifts at the service of one another, each in the measure he has received.

—1 Pt 4:10

REFLECTION. To serve others means to dedicate ourselves to others. It means to have time, strength, hands, and heart for them.

Is my life one of service for others or do I live for myself only?

PRAYER. *My Lord and Savior, let me see You in all human beings, so that I may unselfishly serve You through them.*

MAR. 21

You are "a chosen race, a royal priesthood, a holy nation, a people he claims for his own."

—1 Pt 2:9

REFLECTION. Inalienable property of God—what a great honor but at the same time what a great obligation! Those who wish to belong to God must live in conformity with this high honor; they must lead a holy life.

Do I aspire to this, at least inasmuch as I am able?

PRAYER. *God of majesty, help me to walk ever before You as befits a true child of God.*

But by God's favor I am what I am. —1 Cor 15:10 **MAR. 22**

REFLECTION. These words of St. Paul seem to be filled with pride and presumption but they are really the fruit of humility, for humility is truth.

Humility does not deny one's value or achievements but gives all credit for them to God.

PRAYER. *God of goodness, what would I be without You? Be near me that I may not abuse Your gifts. Let me always show my gratitude for them by leading a Christian life.*

Do you want to be healed? —Jn 5:6 **MAR. 23**

REFLECTION. Our will is necessary for every hour of grace. But it must be an earnest and courageous will, ready for sacrifice.

Then it will open all doors so that grace may enter in and work effectively.

PRAYER. *God of love, You make Your grace depend on my will. Continue to strengthen and guide my will so that my soul may always be open to Your grace.*

MAR. 24 *I know him in whom I have believed.* —2 Tm 1:12

REFLECTION. Why do we fail so often? The underlying reason is that our faith is very weak. It is lacking in power, joy, decisiveness, and victorious certitude.

Yet God Himself is the foundation of faith. In Him is the whole guarantee and defense of salvation.

PRAYER. *Almighty God, let my faith never be shaken by anything, and make all things serve for my salvation.*

MAR. 25 *Mary said: "I am the servant of the Lord."* —Lk 1:38

REFLECTION. What a magnificent program for life! To be a servant of the Lord, that is, to be ever at the disposal of God, ready to regard life with all its joys and sorrows as a sacred mission given us by God's love. And to fulfill this mission with all the generosity of our heart.

Is it really this word of Mary that guides me each day and points out the right way for my life?

PRAYER. *O Mary, faithful servant of the Lord, obtain for me the grace to live as you did, in accord with God's will until death.*

In my Father's house there are many dwelling places. —Jn 14:2

REFLECTION. Our true homeland is heaven. The Father's house is there.

In this world, on the contrary, even the sweetest place must be considered foreign and temporary—a mere stopping off place. Am I aware of this?

PRAYER. *My Savior and my brother, be near me so that the path of my life may always lead me toward heaven.*

In your hands is my destiny. —Ps 31:16

REFLECTION. Everything is in God's hands: my earthly life, its length, its circumstances, everything that happens whether good or bad, its trials and events.

Therefore, my life is in good hands which will protect and guard me with eternal wisdom and love, with lasting faithfulness and mercy. How can I now fear anything?

PRAYER. *My heavenly Father, You always will what is best for me. Guide me to my own good, according to Your will.*

MAR. 28

Therefore I bear with all of this for the sake of those whom God has chosen. —2 Tm 2:10

REFLECTION. Every suffering is a task that God's eternal love sets before human beings. When we patiently endure our troubles, our own soul is enriched and becomes more mature. In addition, we obtain blessings for the souls of others.

I must remember this in the midst of my worries and my sufferings. Then I will not grow weary of carrying my cross or of doing good.

PRAYER. *Father, bless me, and through me let all who draw near me also be blessed.*

MAR. 29

The wages of sin is death, but the gift of God is eternal life in Christ Jesus our Lord. —Rom 6:23

REFLECTION. Eternal death and hell are the punishment due for a life of unrepentant sin. But eternal life that neither begins nor ends with death is God's pure gift and the reward for a life of virtue.

Death or life—I must choose between them. Which shall be my decision?

PRAYER. *Eternal God, I thank You for the gift to choose. Help me to make the right choice.*

Put the spirits to a test to see if they belong to God. —1 Jn 4:1

MAR. 30

REFLECTION. Not everything that shines is gold. What comes from God leads back to Him. Whatever does not lead us to God comes from the devil.

Therefore, I must be prudent and selective in my actions. Do I take care to do this?

PRAYER. *Eternal Wisdom, make me always know and accomplish what is good for my own salvation.*

Make the most of the present opportunity, for these are evil days. —Eph 5:16

MAR. 31

REFLECTION. At every instant God's hour flees away, because time is part of eternity. The time that is wasted is lost for all eternity.

How do I intend to make up for what I have squandered up to now?

PRAYER. *Lord and Father, forgive my negligence and my wicked waste of time. Let me repay my carelessness by doubling my fidelity.*

APR.
1

Then Satan took possession of Judas. —Lk 22:3

REFLECTION. The power of darkness is sinister. It takes its victim even within the circle of Christ's disciples.

However, God will not let us fall—unless we have already opened the doors to the devil. No disciples of Christ betray Him unless they have been vulnerable for a long time. Is everything in me—everything—in order?

PRAYER. *Lord, have pity on me. Do not allow me to fall through impenitence and be lost forever. Let me find my abode in You.*

APR.
2

The reign of God is like yeast. —Mt 13:33

REFLECTION. The yeast of the new life in Christ must permeate the entire inner life of Christians. If we wish to belong to Christ, we must be His completely.

Therefore, there should exist only one thing for me: my total dedication to the faith in all its aspects.

PRAYER. *Lord, keep my eyes ever fixed on You. Let my entire life be dedicated solely to Your service.*

Let me firmly assure you, he who believes has eternal life.—Jn 6:46

APR.
3

REFLECTION. Eternal life is not only something that Christians hope for and expect in the future. It is also something that they actually possess in seed-form in the present.

Those who do not have it now, through a living faith, will not have it after death either. What a duty and responsibility for me!

PRAYER. *Almighty and eternal God, help me to drink daily from Your fountain of grace. Let Your Divine life grow steadily in me.*

You must never grow weary of doing what is right.
—2 Thes 3:13

APR.
4

REFLECTION. All human work can be consecrated and ennobled, because God does not look upon the quantity but the quality of our actions. Everything that we do with a noble and supernatural intention is good.

Do all the actions of my daily life follow this course?

PRAYER. *God of holiness, grant that I may always live for Your glory and thus attain my salvation.*

53

APR. 5

I solemnly assure you, the man who hears my word and has faith in him who sent me possesses eternal life. He does not come under condemnation but has passed from death to life.

—Jn 5:24

REFLECTION. To possess eternal life even now—this is the great promise Christ makes to those who believe in His words, keep them in their heart, and put them into practice.

Those who believe have truly passed from death to life and will avoid condemnation.

PRAYER. *Heavenly Father, Your goodness is my life. Let me serve You until I die.*

———————

APR. 6

If God is for us, who can be against us? —Rom 8:31

REFLECTION. If I am on God's side, then He is also on my side. I can stand with courage against the whole world.

True devotion makes people brave and courageous, sure of their victory.

PRAYER. *Mighty God, strengthen me in Your grace. Let nothing be able to harm me and everything contribute to my good.*

Lose no time; settle with your opponent while on your way to court with him. —Mt 5:25

APR. 7

REFLECTION. God judges us with clemency if He finds in us a mercy that is ready to forgive.

Why do I hesitate in showing mercy to my enemy? For both of us life's road can come to an abrupt end.

PRAYER. *Merciful Savior, help me to show mercy to others, since I hope to receive mercy from You.*

Bear hardship along with me as a good soldier of Christ Jesus. —2 Tm 2:3

APR. 8

REFLECTION. I must put far from me all ways of cowardice and leniency which only seek pleasure and reject all of life's difficulties. The Kingdom of God must endure hardships.

Faith is not a soft cushion but a gift from God for which we must work, struggle, and suffer. I want to reflect on this every day.

PRAYER. *God of mercy, show me the richness of Your love. Free me from all selfishness and let my whole life be dedicated to You that it may bear much fruit.*

APR. 9

Do not yield to grief, like those who have no hope. —1 Thes 4:13

REFLECTION. If everything ended with our death, earthly life would be without hope or comfort. But God does not allow us to vanish into eternal nothingness.

God unites human beings in love and surrounds them with His own love. He does not destroy what He has created but brings it to perfection.

PRAYER. *My God and my Lord, I believe in eternal life because You have promised it.*

APR. 10

Men should regard us as servants of Christ and administrators of the mysteries of God. —1 Cor 4:1

REFLECTION. This is true of all who wish to be true Christians.

I have been entrusted with something very precious: my immortal soul, purchased with the Blood of Christ. Do I take care each day to keep it pure for eternal life?

PRAYER. *Lord, protect my supernatural life against all dangers. Let me remain in Your grace forever.*

The lives of all are to be revealed before the tribunal of Christ so that each one may receive his recompense, good or bad, according to his life in the body.

APR. 11

—2 Cor 5:10

REFLECTION. Earthly life decides a person's life for all eternity.

Everything that I have sown by thought, word, or deed will be my harvest before God's tribunal. What would God's judgment be if I were called before Him this very day?

PRAYER. *Father, make me constant in faith. Help me to produce ripe fruits for heaven.*

Unless you change and become like little children, you will not enter the kingdom of God.

APR. 12

REFLECTION. God reveals Himself as a Father only to those who are like children. Children are free and joyous, innocent and without cares, humble and simple, faithful and trusting.

To become like children, a complete transformation is necessary, one that is able to root out the least selfishness. Do I see in this the principal task of my life?

PRAYER. *Eternal Father, grant me a child's spirit, so that You can love me as Your child.*

APR. 13

Do not judge, and you will not be judged. —Lk 6:37

REFLECTION. How often our conscience is lax in judging ourselves while our heart is strict in judging the failings of others! The opposite should be the case.

Even if my reason can accuse, my kind heart must defend and Christian charity must be the judge. This will lead to a judgment of love, which will one day obtain for me a merciful judgment from God.

PRAYER. *Father, be kind and merciful toward me and toward all humankind.*

APR. 14

Whoever is of God hears every word God speaks. —Jn 8:47

REFLECTION. God still speaks to us today. His voice can be heard in all the events of life—not only the important ones but the insignificant ones as well.

However, His voice is heard only by those who are aware of Divine things and have not become insensible through their worldly ties. Whom do I listen to?

PRAYER. *My Father, help me to hear Your voice when You speak to me. Grant that I may always answer with joy.*

While we live we are responsible to the Lord, and when we die we die as his servants. Both in life and in death we are the Lord's.
—Rom 14:8

APR. 15

REFLECTION. We belong to the Lord both in life and in death! This gives every human life a particular meaning, a particular goal, and also a special dedication.

It casts a comforting and victorious light on every suffering, every sadness, and every trial.

PRAYER. *Good Father, let me never forget that I am always completely Yours.*

We are afflicted in every way possible, but we are not crushed; full of doubts, we never despair.
—2 Cor 4:8

APR. 16

REFLECTION. This Scripture passage contains a wonderful and victorious "but," with which the Apostle conquers all the difficulties of life. In spite of his weakness, he feels strong; in spite of his poverty, rich; in spite of his frailty, victorious.

Why? Because God is with him. Those who have God have everything.

PRAYER. *O Lord, I carry You deep in my heart. Be with me until the end of my days.*

59

APR. 17

Do you want to leave me too?

—Jn 6:67

REFLECTION. What does God lose if I leave Him? Nothing. He does not need me.

But I lose everything if I stray away from Him—everything for time and for eternity. And what does this do to me?

PRAYER. *My God, You are my happiness and my life. Let me always be near You and let me serve You faithfully, even though sometimes I may not succeed in seeing and understanding You.*

APR. 18

Blessed are they who have not seen and have believed.

—Jn 20:29

REFLECTION. To see and believe is not difficult. However, believing without seeing is only possible when one is deeply convinced of the existence of an omnipotent God.

Thus faith becomes the heroic part of our life. Do I have this faith?

PRAYER. *My good Father, I believe firmly in Your eternal omnipotence, in Your wisdom, and in Your love. Increase my faith.*

The love of God has been poured in our hearts through the Holy Spirit who has been given to us.
—Rom 5:5

APR.
19

REFLECTION. God's Spirit and love are one and the same. When there is no love, the Holy Spirit is not present.

However, where the Holy Spirit reigns, the love of God and of our neighbor also flourishes. This gives me food for much thought.

PRAYER. *Holy Spirit, enkindle the hearts of the faithful with the fire of Your love.*

We have this confidence in God: that he hears us whenever we ask for anything according to his will.
—1 Jn 5:14

APR.
20

REFLECTION. "According to His will"—this is the important thing to remember when we pray and the ultimate reason why certain prayers are not heard.

When the selfish human will opposes God's will, the prayer is useless.

PRAYER. *My Lord and my God, give me always only what is good for my salvation. Do so even if it is not what I think is good for me.*

61

APR. 21

Woe to you scribes and Pharisees, you frauds! You are like white-washed tombs. —Mt 23:27

REFLECTION. My life overflows with works of God's Divine grace and mercy. Have I always heeded His voice and have I always benefited from His grace?

Neglected grace becomes a judgment against me. I must never forget this.

PRAYER. *My God and my Father, let me see everything in Your light, and help me always to do Your will.*

APR. 22

Be solicitous to make your call and election permanent . . . surely those who do so will never be lost. —2 Pt 1:10

REFLECTION. God has called and predestined me for eternal happiness. However, I may fail to obtain it through my own fault.

I must conform my life to this call and, through prayer and the sacraments, make sure of my predestination. Do I make an effort to do this?

PRAYER. *Lord, You have given me a good start. Let me also have a good end.*

If you understood the meaning of the text, "It is mercy I desire and not sacrifice," you would not have condemned innocent men.
—Mt 12:7

APR. 23

REFLECTION. Taking pride in one's virtue without piety is an abomination in God's eyes.

All sacrifices and acts of devotion are vain if those who practice them lack compassion for their neighor. The most essential thing is missing: love.

PRAYER. *Just God, grant me Your mercy. Let me also show mercy to others, even when it is hard for me to do so.*

When you fast, see to it that you groom your hair and wash your face. In that way no one can see you are fasting but your Father who is hidden.
—Mt 6:17

APR. 24

REFLECTION. The spiritual life is too sacred and intimate to be paraded before others. It is only between God and the soul.

Any other motive—even if it is only the desire to be pitied or recognized—destroys everything.

PRAYER. *My Father, let me always seek You alone. Help me to give You honor and receive Your approval.*

**APR.
25**

You are not judging by God's standards but by man's.

—Mt 16:23

REFLECTION. Peter is reproved because in his zeal he wants to turn the Lord aside from His sorrowful way. This reproval can be directed to me also!

Do I not prefer to work for God rather than to suffer or shed my blood for Him? Yet only one way leads to Him—the way of the Cross.

PRAYER. *My crucified Lord, grant me a sincere love for the Cross. May I one day partake of its blessings.*

**APR.
26**

Therefore, live in Christ Jesus the Lord, in the spirit in which you received him.

—Col 2:6

REFLECTION. The "Yes" of the baptismal promises obliges us to be faithful until death. Yet, how often this "Yes" contrasts vividly with the "No" of our daily lives!

I must take seriously my duty to walk with Jesus. This means I must follow Him along every way—even the way of the Cross.

PRAYER. *My heavenly Father, grant me the spirit of Christ. Whether in joy or in sorrow let me walk in accord with Your wish.*

Master, we have been hard at it all night long and have caught nothing; but if you say so, I will lower the nets. —Lk 5:5

APR. 27

REFLECTION. It is a sad lot to work in vain! Yet it also means to hope against hope, and to have confidence in God, even in the most bitter hour of discouragement and delusion.

God's word and His blessings will create something new even from apparent ruin. Why do I forget this?

PRAYER. *My Lord and my God, I trust in You. Let me humbly and devoutly submit myself to Your holy will.*

You are the temple of the living God. —2 Cor 6:16

APR. 28

REFLECTION. I am the temple of God. This means not only great dignity, a fullness of grace and blessing, but also a fullness of responsibility.

If I am the temple of the living God, nothing profane must be in me. What things, therefore, should I put away from my heart that God may dwell in me?

PRAYER. *Holy Spirit, turn to me and fill me with Your grace. Let me live a holy life and be pleasing to You.*

APR. 29

My little children, be on your guard against idols. —1 Jn 5:21

REFLECTION. The world knows many idols which it serves. Some of them are: power, esteem, money, pleasure, ambition, and passion for another person or for one's own "ego."

The true Christian knows and senses only one: Christ, only Christ, the total Christ. Whom or what do I serve the most?

PRAYER. *My Lord and Savior, free me from every worldly spirit. Let me follow You with faithfulness and total dedication.*

APR. 30

It was not you who chose me, it was I who chose you. —Jn 15:16

REFLECTION. For what I am and have I give thanks to the one and only God. His faithful grace is always with me in everything.

This should inspire in me not only a sincere humility and a spirit of filial gratitude, but also the desire to hold fast to God's outstretched hand, so that none of His graces may be fruitless in me. Is this true in my case?

PRAYER. *Merciful God, I give You thanks for all the graces of my life. Carry to fulfillment all that You have begun in me.*

My being proclaims the greatness of the Lord. **MAY**
—Lk 1:26 **1**

REFLECTION. This is the answer of the Mother of God to the greeting of her cousin Elizabeth. There is for Mary a central point around which her whole person, her whole being, moves— God, the Lord. She refers to Him everything, even the praises given to her.

Do I act likewise?

PRAYER. *My God and my All!*

Nobody sews a piece of unshrunken cloth on an old coat. **MAY**
—Mt 9:16 **2**

REFLECTION. The old and the new "unshrunken," flesh and the spirit, are incompatible. Therefore, any reconciliation between them is useless.

If, according to God's wishes, one must become a new self, then the old, earthly self must first be eliminated through prayer, penance, and a complete inner transformation.

PRAYER. *Lord, create in me a new heart, a new spirit, and a new understanding. Let me ever rejoice in You.*

MAY 3

You don't know to what spirit you belong.
—Lk 9:55 (Vulgate not NAB)

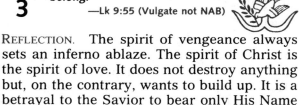

REFLECTION. The spirit of vengeance always sets an inferno ablaze. The spirit of Christ is the spirit of love. It does not destroy anything but, on the contrary, wants to build up. It is a betrayal to the Savior to bear only His Name and not His spirit.

Do I earnestly try to obtain this Spirit?

PRAYER. *My Savior, let me love others as You have loved them—unto death.*

MAY 4

The command I give you is this, that you love one another.
—Jn 15:17

REFLECTION. Isn't love a natural thing? Then why make it a commandment? Because of our great selfishness. Truly, selfishness is the death of love.

Now, a disinterested soul may love those who have nothing lovable about them. The rewards of a disinterested love will never be lacking.

PRAYER. *Spirit of love, let me sow love, so that some day I may harvest it.*

How hard it is for the rich to enter the kingdom of God!—Mk 10:23

MAY 5

REFLECTION. Riches cause people to become weak, sated, and lazy.

How can such individuals have a total dedication to God if they have never learned from the hard school of life how to make sacrifices and deny themselves!

PRAYER. *Lord, the way that leads to Your Kingdom is narrow and steep. Help me to traverse it to the end.*

He has looked upon his servant in her lowliness. —Lk 1:48

MAY 6

REFLECTION. This passage shows the moving humility on the part of God's young Mother! Are not the good things that we have, in the last analysis, a free gift from the eternal love, a look of grace from the eyes of the Father?

Therefore, what a stream of humble gratitude should constantly flow from our hearts!

PRAYER. *O Mary, humble servant of the Lord, thank Your Son for all the graces of my life. Help me to express my thanks by a life that is pleasing to God.*

MAY 7

Should anyone press you into service for one mile, go with him for two miles. —Mt 5:41

REFLECTION. Nothing helps so much to build up the Kingdom of God as disinterested love. Therefore, be always ready to render a service of love, even when it entails sacrifice. Try to place the welfare of others before your own.

If you wish to be a true Christian, love must distinguish you from those who are not Christians.

PRAYER. *My Savior, let me see You in my neighbor and serve You in him.*

MAY 8

How can... you accept praise from one another yet do not seek the glory that comes from God? —Jn 5:44

REFLECTION. Ambition is one of the greatest obstacles to faith. How can persons with absolute faithfulness and the brave spirit of a confessor be on God's side if they are still concerned with the opinions of others and seek human praise?

From whom do I see praise—God or human beings?

PRAYER. *My Lord and my God, make me abhor the spirit of worldliness. Let me aspire to live according only to what is pleasing to You.*

There is no greater love than this: to lay down one's life for one's friends. —Jn 15:13

MAY 9

REFLECTION. Sacrifice is the touchstone, love's supreme test. Love is true only when it can face sacrifice.

What would be the result of this test in me? Is my love ready to make any sacrifice?

PRAYER. *Most loving Savior, grant me a love ready to do anything, even the greatest sacrifice, that I may become Your true disciple.*

She gave from her want, all that she had to live on. —Mk 12:44

MAY 10

REFLECTION. God measures, weighs, and judges differently from us humans. He does not consider what people give as the most important thing, but what the object given means to them.

This is the best measure of love, the only thing that has value in God's sight.

PRAYER. *God of love, You have given me everything, including Yourself. I want to give You everything I have.*

MAY 11 *Let your belts be fastened around your waists and your lamps be burning ready.* —Lk 12:35

REFLECTION. There is only one cure for the highs and lows of our inner life: to be always ready.

Am I ready to be taken at any moment before the Lord to be judged? Even right now?

PRAYER. *Heavenly Father, let me live in such a way that I will be ready at any moment to come before Your tribunal with confidence.*

MAY 12 *God who is mighty has done great things for me.* —Lk 1:49

REFLECTION. Acknowledgment of true greatness does not conflict with the spirit of humility—for humility is truth. Humble persons do not call great what is little or black what is white. They give glory to God for every good gift.

Do I always seek to be truly humble in this way?

PRAYER. *Lord, protect me from vain complacency and from presumption. Never let me lose Your benevolence.*

He who sows bountifully will reap bountifully. —2 Cor 9:6

MAY 13

REFLECTION. Never think of your personal benefit when you give.

God pays back in a truly royal manner what a disinterested love gives.

PRAYER. *Lord, I want to love You and love my neighbor for Your sake, because You are the highest, the most loving good.*

Beg the harvest master to send out laborers to gather his harvest. —Mt 9:38

MAY 14

REFLECTION. Sending out laborers is up to God. But it is our task to pray that they be sent out. That is why each of us is bound at least to pray for the missions, even if we cannot personally be sent there.

Do I still have a sense of God's cause, of His harvest—or am I concerned only with my own interests?

PRAYER. *Heavenly Father, grant that Your will may always be my will also.*

MAY 15

Have no love for the world, nor the things that the world affords.
—1 Jn 2:15

REFLECTION. This seems to be a renunciation of life but it is really an affirmation of true life. God wants to pull me away from the nothingness and fleeting character of the world, so that my heart will not go astray.

Why am I so attached to the pettiness of earth that I neglect the only thing necessary?

PRAYER. *Father, grant that You alone will be the object of my love, my fidelity.*

MAY 16

Whatever you do—you should do all for the glory of God.
—1 Cor 10:31

REFLECTION. Even secular things can and should be enlisted in the holy service of God. Put your whole life, even your joys, into the cup of a right intention, and then everything will contribute to the glory of God and obtain a blessing for you!

Do I begin each day in this spirit?

PRAYER. *Lord, bless everything I think, say, do, and suffer, so that it may acquire eternal value.*

Give your service willingly, doing it for the Lord rather than men.
—Eph 6:7

MAY 17

REFLECTION. Those who serve human beings alone make human beings the judges of their conduct, and therefore they are concerned only with external success.

But those who serve God can do so only with all of their energies, with complete fidelity, love, and dedication, even in the smallest and least significant things.

PRAYER. *Lord, free me from human respect and ostentation. Let my whole life be consecrated only to Your service.*

He has shown might with his arm.
—Lk 1:51

MAY 18

REFLECTION. The history of the world is neither the work of human beings nor the playground for a blind fate. It is the work of God. Everything that happens is subordinated to the laws of eternal Power and Wisdom.

This joyous news of Divine Providence should infuse me with boundless confidence and banish all pessimism.

PRAYER. *Omnipotent and all-perfect God, I trust in You. Let Your will be done in me.*

MAY 19 *Whoever wants to rank first among you must serve the needs of all.* —Mt 20:26

REFLECTION. In the kingdom of the world, success and ambition are what count; each person is a neighbor only to himself or herself.

But the opposite is true in the Kingdom of God: the only recognized nobility is to serve with humility.

PRAYER. *God of goodness, do not let me forget that as I become more closely united with You I will be better able to see and love You in my neighbor.*

MAY 20 *If the Son frees you, you will really be free.* —Jn 8:36

REFLECTION. Many chains can bind a person: worldly pleasures, human respect, fear of suffering, or the fear of death.

Christ has taken away all these chains and has given a totally different meaning and purpose to life. Whoever accepts Christ's freedom is truly free and happy.

PRAYER. *Lord, bind me to You and never permit anything to separate me from You.*

Observe everything they tell you. But do not follow their example.
—Mt 23:3

MAY 21

REFLECTION. Whoever hides unholy deeds under pious words is a Pharisee and rejected by God. It is not enough to teach the truth and fight for it; it is also necessary to live according to it. Doctrine and life must go together.

Is this so in my life?

PRAYER. *My Savior, let me set a Christian example for others in all things.*

Why do you criticize this woman? It is a good deed she has done for me.
—Mt 26:10

MAY 22

REFLECTION. To show love for neighbor is never a waste. True piety is revelation of the immense, overflowing love of God. It knows neither greed nor cupidity.

Do I have in me this piety that acts through love?

PRAYER. *Heavenly Father, You have given us Your Son as a precious gift. In exchange take from me everything that I have.*

MAY 23

He said to the disciple, "There is your mother!" —Jn 19:27

REFLECTION. This Bible passage shows how the communication between two souls is created. They are bound together by their common love for Christ.

The communion at the foot of the Cross is the true communion guaranteed to last forever. It purifies and strengthens, transfigures and sanctifies, because it is blessed by the Crucified Lord!

PRAYER. *My Savior, let me consider every tie to another creature as a gift that You have bestowed on me.*

———————————

MAY 24

All of you are children of light and of the day. —1 Thes 5:5

REFLECTION. What a wonderful grace this is: I too can be a child of the day, the new day that has dawned for the world in Christ!

Do I strive to carry this light to those who still languish in the sadness and oppression of the night, so that they may find their way to the dwelling of the Father in light inaccessible?

PRAYER. *Lord, I pray to You for all creatures. Guide them to Your eternal dwelling place.*

He who lives in me and I in him, will produce abundantly.

—Jn 15:5

MAY 25

REFLECTION. The secret of producing good spiritual fruit lies in union with God. If this union is destroyed through sin and we are separated from God, then—in spite of all natural actions and efforts—we will be barren.

How do I stand in this respect?

PRAYER. *Heavenly Father, take away from me anything that hinders my spiritual growth.*

In hope we were saved.

—Rom 8:24

MAY 26

REFLECTION. The consequences of sin have not yet been eliminated; the powers of darkness are always at work. We have not arrived at our destination but are still on our way.

Yet in the night of our weakness there shines the brilliant light of the hope that God Himself will perfect in His faithful the work that He has begun in them.

PRAYER. *Lord Jesus Christ, let Your grace supply everything that I lack.*

MAY 27

Come to me, all you who are weary . . . and I will refresh you.
—Mt 11:28

REFLECTION. In the midst of life's burdens there is one comfort only: the immense depth of God's love that renews us even when human comfort falls short.

The only thing the Lord asks is that we go to Him. Why then do I go to creatures and not to Him?

PRAYER. *Most loving Savior, let me find in You everything that I need for soul and body.*

MAY 28

A man . . . came out looking for fruit [from his fig tree] but did not find any.
—Lk 13:16

REFLECTION. God does not want grapes from the fig tree, just as He does not ask any of us to accomplish something that is beyond our possibilities, strength, or ability.

However, God does demand fruit. If we are chosen and found barren, we will be cast out.

PRAYER. *My God and my Father, do not allow Your grace to be wasted in me.*

The last shall come first.

—Mt 19:30

MAY 29

REFLECTION. A good beginning is not enough. We must keep on going from day to day through our daily struggles in order to guarantee that our end will also be good.

With God's grace the last can become first, by turning back to Him fully repentant. But woe to those who were first yet through their own neglect have become the last!

PRAYER. *Lord, grant me patience and perseverance. Let my initial enthusiasm not diminish in me but lead me happily to my end.*

Through [the Cross] . . . I [have been crucified] to the world.

—Gal 6:14

MAY 30

REFLECTION. Only one attitude leads to the freeing of the "self" and prevents inordinate attachment to the things of the world: the ever-renewed humble turning to the Crucified Lord.

In the light of the Cross, everything else fades away. Why do I evade this light?

PRAYER. *Most lovable Jesus, You died for me on the Cross. Make me die to everything that does not lead me to You.*

MAY 31 *They did not grasp what he said to them.* —Lk 2:50

REFLECTION. Not even the greatest faith in God can illuminate all the darkness that surrounds His designs or way of acting.

Therefore, it is good for us to imitate Mary—to fold our hands and bow before the inscrutable word of God. God never deceives a trusting faith.

PRAYER. *Heavenly Father, let Your ways be ever mine also. I want to follow You always, even if this should mean to walk in darkness and in need.*

JUNE 1 *What I am doing is sending you out like sheep among wolves.* —Mt 10:16

REFLECTION. The nature of the wolf will always be in the world. Whoever howls with the world is the friend of the world and the enemy of God.

Woe to you if in the world you have only friends!

PRAYER. *O Good Shepherd, You have placed me in this world. Grant that I may not follow its ways, but that I may always follow You.*

Examine yourselves. Perhaps you yourselves do not realize that Christ Jesus is in you.

JUNE 2

—2 Cor 13:5

REFLECTION. There is an infallible sign by which I can recognize if my faith is genuine—if Christ is in me and rules my entire life!

Is the reason for my frequent lapses my lack of a living faith?

PRAYER. *Lord, be always with me. Direct and guide my whole life according to Your holy will.*

Lord, if you had been here, my brother would never have died.

JUNE 3

REFLECTION. Faith is not a guarantee of safe conduct against life's adversities. It does not impose any duties upon God—only upon human beings.

In my attitude toward God, is not the opposite true at times?

PRAYER. *Lord, strengthen my faith.*

JUNE 4 *If you can trust a man in little things, you can also trust him in greater.* —Lk 16:10

REFLECTION. The extraordinary deeds which meet with human applause and give satisfaction to a person's vanity are easy to accomplish. The silent faithfulness in doing the little daily duties that no one sees or considers is much harder!

Yet the strength to accomplish great things arises precisely from faithful perseverance in little things.

PRAYER. *Heavenly Father, You have given me all Your love. Help me to serve You with absolute faith and dedication.*

JUNE 5 *Not on bread alone is man to live but on every utterance that comes from the mouth of God.* —Mt 4:4

REFLECTION. Human beings have the Divine life in them. Woe to them if that life languishes or is extinguished. As the body needs daily nourishment, so the soul needs every word that God shows through the duties and events of each day.

Do I always pay attention to this?

PRAYER. *My Father, make me understand always what You say, and accomplish what You wish.*

We have put aside everything to follow you!
—Mk 10:28

JUNE 6

REFLECTION. Nothing is given to God as a free gift. He gives us infinitely more than what He receives from us.

Why do I hesitate then to sacrifice myself for Him?

PRAYER. *Lord, You are infinitely good. Let me be moved by Your infinite love so that I may be ready to make any sacrifice for Your love.*

Sir, leave it another year.
—Lk 13:8

JUNE 7

REFLECTION. God sees fruits from my life; He gives me time for this. But the time of grace passes and then comes the judgment.

What would God's judgment of me be today?

PRAYER. *Just God, be patient with me. Do not let me die before my life has borne fruit for You.*

JUNE 8

Is it permitted to do a good deed on the sabbath—or an evil one? To preserve life—or to destroy it?
—Mk 3:4

REFLECTION. God has created life and He wishes it to be preserved.

Whoever harms a person's life or health—either by human rules or laws or even by following sacred practices or pious habits—sins against God's creative will.

PRAYER. *God of greatness, do not let me ever oppose Your will because of mere human laws. You are above everything, even above human laws.*

———————

JUNE 9

My mission is to spread, not peace, but division.
—Mt 10:34

REFLECTION. A lazy and comfortable life is not suited for the struggles against the evil in this world. This requires great solicitude and total dedication.

When Christ calls there is nothing else we can do but obey Him. Am I ready for this?

PRAYER. *Lord, You have called me. Let me always be a faithful and brave apostle for You.*

*Why do you call me "Lord, Lord,"
and not put into practice what I
teach you?* —Lk 6:46

**JUNE
10**

REFLECTION. For Jesus, it is of no value if we confess Him with our lips. We must also live according to His word. He does not wish any external homage, but the fulfillment of His Father's will.

Is this my daily aspiration?

PRAYER. *My Savior, grant me the deep conviction that there is only one way to go to the Father: the fulfillment of His holy will!*

Whoever acknowledges me before men I will acknowledge before my Father in heaven.
—Mt 10:32

**JUNE
11**

REFLECTION. There is no love without sorrows, nor an imitation of Jesus without ignominy.

Beware of the desire to keep the world's friendship at any cost. This only results in the denial of Christ. Whoever are ashamed to confess Him are traitors and destroy their faith.

PRAYER. *Lord, even if everybody should be unfaithful, I will remain ever faithful to You, so that gratitude will not perish on earth.*

JUNE 12

Rejoice . . . that your names are inscribed in heaven. —Lk 10:20

REFLECTION. To be great in this world and to do things is not what matters, but rather to be pleasing before God. Do not let yourself be inebriated with the glory of earthly pleasures and possessions.

Try to be humble and simple like a child. The kingdom of heaven has been promised to those simple souls who are like children.

PRAYER. *My good Father, give me the love and simplicity of a child so that I may be worthy of Your love.*

JUNE 13

He who brings himself to nought for me discovers who he is. —Mt 10:39

REFLECTION. Love of life is not in itself an evil, but if exaggerated it becomes a poisonous vulgar selfishness. Eternal life in God is found only by those who are dead to the base life of selfishness.

Am I resolved to do this, at any cost?

PRAYER. *Lord, give me the strength to sacrifice everything for You, so that in doing so I may become worthy of You.*

Lord, would you not have us call down fire from heaven to destroy them? —Lk 9:54 **JUNE 14**

REFLECTION. Wrath is profane and impious. It is an alien fire on the altar of the heart.

True disciples of Christ must never let themselves be consumed by the fire of anger, but always be guided by their Divine nobility. Then they will have passed the test by fire.

PRAYER. *Most loving Savior, teach me to be meek and humble so that I will never offend against charity.*

The Son of Man has not come to be served but to serve. —Mk 10:45 **JUNE 15**

REFLECTION. One of the most dangerous temptations for human beings is ambition. It can be conquered only by the spirit of Christ, that is, the spirit of love—dedication to the service of others.

Do I have this dedication? Am I, like Christ, a candle that consumes itself to illumine others?

PRAYER. *Jesus, my brother, give me a disinterested love, one that is ready to make any sacrifice.*

JUNE 16

Birds . . . do not sow or reap . . . yet your heavenly Father feeds them.
—Mt 6:26

REFLECTION. Birds are some of God's creatures that do not reason; nevertheless, He feeds them.

We also are God's children. Can we not rightly expect from our Father everything that we need? Put away fear, timidity, and anguished preoccupation.

PRAYER. *My Father, I trust that You will give me everything I need, whether for my soul or for my body.*

JUNE 17

We must do the deeds of him who sent me while it is day. The night comes on when no one can work.
—Jn 9:4

REFLECTION. The sowing time is limited. Those who do not take advantage of it will reap in vain.

How do I work? Do I work constantly yet without anxiety?

PRAYER. *Lord, may Your blessings descend upon me always and upon my work. Help me to be Your good and faithful servant forever.*

There are different gifts but the same Spirit. —1 Cor 12:4

JUNE 18

REFLECTION. Nobody has everything and nobody can do everything—neither in the natural nor in the supernatural life. Therefore, do not be envious if your brother or sister Christian has received more than you.

Be thankful for the different gifts given by the Holy Spirit and see that the talents given to you bear fruit in the best possible manner. All faithfulness will meet its Divine reward.

PRAYER. *Creator of heaven and earth, grant that I may become whatever You wish.*

Only the one who does the will of my Father [will enter the Kingdom of God]. —Mt 7:21

JUNE 19

REFLECTION. There is no value whatever in any of our external religious actions unless we also have an internal willingness to satisfy the demands of God.

To believe that we can avoid the serious duties of obedience is a vain attempt to escape God's judgment.

PRAYER. *My Lord and my Savior, You were obedient unto death. Grant me to be similarly obedient to Your Father's will.*

JUNE 20

You shall love your neighbor as yourself. —Lk 10:27

REFLECTION. Those who are wholly devoted to God know that they really love the heavenly Father only when they serve Him in their brothers and sisters here on earth.

Therefore, they will not only try to avoid anything that may wound charity. They will also seek and make opportunities to show their love to others.

PRAYER. *O eternal Love, make me love You in all creatures as You wish and deserve.*

JUNE 21

To me, "life" means Christ. —Phil 1:21

REFLECTION. A life without Christ is a life without value. It is He alone Who frees us from guilt and sin. He gives us the Divine life of grace and introduces us to communion with the Father, in the unity of the Holy Spirit.

But this new life in Christ is possible only when the old sinful self, which leads us to perdition, is completely dead.

PRAYER. *Jesus, for You I live, and for You I die. Jesus, I am Yours in life and in death.*

Put away ambitious thoughts and associate with those who are lowly. —Rom 12:16

JUNE 22

REFLECTION. Do not wait for the time when you may accomplish great things. By doing so you will only be wasting time and living on the fringe of life.

Reality is made up of a thousand little things. Do them seriously because this is the only right way to make our lives truly great.

PRAYER. *Lord, give me Your great love. Then the honor I give You daily will also be great.*

You refused me! —Lk 13:34

JUNE 23

REFLECTION. God has placed only one condition on His will to dispense grace: the free will of human beings. No one is forced to go to heaven. However, those who desire to do so and who carry out God's will for them are readily taken care of.

Therefore, I must let nothing prevent me from aspiring to it with all my strength.

PRAYER. *Heavenly Father, enlighten my mind and strengthen my will. Let me acknowledge You as my supreme good and ask for nothing other than You.*

JUNE 24 *I do not ask you to take them out of the world, but to guard them from the evil one.* —Jn 17:15

REFLECTION.   Christ does not take away from those who belong to Him their struggles and crosses. But He prays for them so that they will not perish.

This thought should fill me with great courage. I am not alone; Christ is with me, my Divine Brother.

PRAYER.   *My Savior, held by Your hand I can easily ascend to the heights of a holy life. Stay at my side that I may never fail to obtain this.*

JUNE 25 *Why did the fig tree wither up so quickly?* —Mt 21:30

REFLECTION.   Fruitless and barren is all devotion that is merely an external practice and lacks an inner meaning. It is comprised of dead leaves without fruit.

Where the breath of the spirit is not present, where love is lacking, anything no matter how small may stop its work. Do I strive to obtain true compassion?

PRAYER.   *My Father, help me so that my whole being and all my actions may be a song of love rendering glory and honor to You.*

The Son of Man has nowhere to lay his head. —Lk 9:58

JUNE 26

REFLECTION. Poor, without a home, tired and weary, without human security . . . such was the Master's life. And such will be the lives of those who wish to follow Him in fidelity.

Am I frightened by this kind of life? Why?

PRAYER. *My Savior and Redeemer, You are the only way to the Father. Help me so that I may walk in this Way.*

Christ died for all so that those who live might live no longer for themselves but for him. —2 Cor 5:15

JUNE 27

REFLECTION. To live for oneself means to say "no" to God. To live for Christ means to live as He has lived.

The motto of His life was: "For you." The motto of my own life should be: "For Christ." Is this really the case?

PRAYER. *My Savior, I wish to offer my whole life to Your service and that of my brothers and sisters. Let me be completely Yours.*

JUNE 28

No pupil outranks his teacher, no slave his master. —Mt 10:24

REFLECTION. To be Jesus' disciple means to have a special mission in the world; it means to be subject only to the authoritative commandments of the Teacher. The true disciples willingly share the Passion of Christ, for without a common fate with the Lord, there is no common life with Him.

Am I afraid of this kind of loving commitment?

PRAYER. *Lord, give me the strength to endure the sufferings that it is Your will I must endure. Let me bear my cross without complaint.*

———————————

JUNE 29

My yoke is easy and my burden light. —Mt 11:30

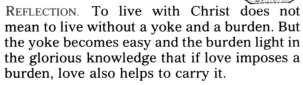

REFLECTION. To live with Christ does not mean to live without a yoke and a burden. But the yoke becomes easy and the burden light in the glorious knowledge that if love imposes a burden, love also helps to carry it.

Hence, those who have been redeemed are always happy, even under the weight of the Cross. Am I among these?

PRAYER. *My Savior, You are my whole happiness and life. I give You thanks from my heart, even though Your love for me must be manifest in the Cross.*

96

Is it lawful to cure on the sab- **JUNE**
bath?
—Lk 14:3
30

REFLECTION. How many times love is hindered by a mere ruling that should be, in all truth, helping it! This is not God's will.

Love should be above any other commandment, for it is the greatest. Is this the norm in my life and in my relations with others?

PRAYER. *Most loving Savior, give me the desire to serve others with love and to offer myself for them, as You have offered Yourself for me.*

Anyone unjust in a slight matter **JULY**
is also unjust in greater.
—Lk 16:10
1

REFLECTION. Constant dishonesty in little things dulls the soul and blunts the conscience. More and more it blocks our relations with God.

An unfaithful manager thinks only of himself; an honest one thinks of his employer. Of whom do I think?

PRAYER. *Merciful God, forgive all the infidelities of my life. Help me to atone for them with an increased fidelity.*

JULY 2

You cannot give yourself to God and money. —Mt 6:24

REFLECTION. To serve God means to live completely and wholly for God. To live for money means to abandon oneself to the things of this world and to one's own personal interests. One service excludes the other.

Those who think they can serve both God and the goods of this world will suffer the sad consequences of such delusion.

PRAYER. *Eternal God, protect me from a false worldly piety. At the same time, also keep me from a weak and lifeless Christianity. I want to be all Yours!*

JULY 3

Let us profess the truth in love and grow to the full maturity of Christ the head. —Eph 4:15

REFLECTION. Truth without love offends; love without truth deceives. Therefore, whoever wishes to grow in interior spirit and to be free from deceit and selfishness must strive to obtain both truth and love.

This is life's central point and the assurance of a constant inner growth.

PRAYER. *Lord, make my love pure and strong, and sanctify it with Your truth.*

With God there is no favoritism.
—Rom 2:11

JULY 4

REFLECTION. Superficial people are easily deceived by social rank and wealth, that is, by external appearances. But God looks at the heart, not at externals.

Nobody can deceive Him by applying an external varnish to the impurity that lies underneath. What shame is brought on by our arrogance and haughtiness!

PRAYER. *Eternal Father, make me great in humility and love. Only then will I be truly great before You.*

One among you is your teacher, the rest are learners [brothers and sisters].
—Mt 23:8

JULY 5

REFLECTION. In spite of all human distinction we are all ultimately on a common level. We are all brothers and sisters under the one Teacher.

With this thought in mind, how simple become all relations among us! All deviations and animosity are put to flight!

PRAYER. *My Lord and my Savior, give me a fraternal love for all those whom You love. They are both Your brothers and sisters and mine.*

JULY 6

Even if my life is to be poured out as a libation over the sacrificial service of your faith, I am glad of it.
—Phil 2:17

REFLECTION. What I do and suffer benefits not only me but also others. In the economy of grace we can be of mutual help to one another.

This holy communion and mutual aid cannot help but bring true peace and contentment to the soul.

PRAYER. *Lord, make me constant in my prayers and sacrifices. Let my life be fruitful not only for me but also for my brothers and sisters.*

JULY 7

Join me in the struggle by your prayers to God in my behalf.
—Rom 15:30

REFLECTION. The work in the Kingdom of God is a struggle against the powers of darkness. To pray for the workers and join with them is to collaborate in the struggle for victory.

I too want to make my contribution to this effort every day of my life!

PRAYER. *Almighty God, make me share Your strength. Grant that in spite of any personal trials, I may never forget or neglect the great concerns of Your Church.*

I can never be alone; the Father is with me. —Jn 16:32

JULY 8

REFLECTION. Even when it seemed that He had been forsaken by His Father, Christ was not alone. The Father was always with Him because He was in the Father.

Thus, I too will never be abandoned and alone in either life or death if I do not stray voluntarily away from God by sin. Could I ever be foolish enough to do such a thing?

PRAYER. *Dearest Father, Your grace is my only hope. Make me always conscious that You are near me.*

Where your treasure is, there your heart is also. —Mt 6:21

JULY 9

REFLECTION. Wealth may bring happiness, but it is also a danger, since it easily leads to greed, making one forget the true eternal good. Only one thing removes this danger— total dedication to Christ.

Whenever the Lords fills the heart it is easier to reject the danger of temporal things. What is the object of my thoughts and to what am I attracted?

PRAYER. *My Savior, make me all Yours and make me happy in Your love.*

JULY 10

Fear not and do not stand in awe of what this people fears.

—1 Pt 3:14

REFLECTION. All human fears have been taken away! If God is with me, who can stand against me?

He is more powerful than the world and the powers of evil. Even my enemies must submit to Him.

PRAYER. *Omnipotent God, Lord of heaven and earth, clothe me with the fullness of Your strength. Without fear or hesitation may I walk in all the ways through which You lead me.*

JULY 11

But I have prayed for you that your faith may never fail.

—Lk 22:32

REFLECTION. The last and strongest tie that binds us to God is faith. Everything depends upon it. Those who believe may fall, but they are never lost. Even when sinners fall away from God's merciful arms, they still can hope for forgiveness, as long as they have not cut this last tie with Him.

PRAYER. *Merciful God and Father, never let me stray away from You. Then neither will You abandon me.*

For to you I have entrusted my cause!
—Jer 12:20

JULY 12

REFLECTION. To place ourselves and all that we have in the hands of God means freedom amid chains. It means victory amid certain defeat. It signifies life even in death.

Who hinders me from dedicating myself wholly to God?

PRAYER. *Eternal God, You know all things. Do with me what You will.*

I am not worthy to have you under my roof.
—Mt 8:8

JULY 13

REFLECTION. Those who say from the bottom of their heart: "I am not worthy, because I am nothing," are on the best path to union with God.

In fact, they are already with God, because God goes out to meet the humble heart.

PRAYER. *Jesus, meek and humble of heart, make my own heart like to Yours.*

JULY 14

If anyone wishes to rank first, he must remain the last one and the servant of all. —Mk 9:35

REFLECTION. Haughtiness and ambition are deeply rooted in human nature. It is only through willing and loving humble service that these basic defects may be rooted out.

Even Christ, in order "to reign," had to serve first.

PRAYER. *My Lord and Master, open my heart to my brothers and sisters. Teach me the secret of serving them with humility, so that I may always become more like You.*

JULY 15

Did I not assure you that if you believed you would see the glory of God displayed? —Jn 11:40

REFLECTION. Above all things and every reality stands the promise of God as the most powerful of all. Those who believe in that promise can count on the impossible—even miracles.

For God never goes back on His Word—He is eternal faithfulness. What can possibly lead me to doubt?

PRAYER. *Heavenly Father, You help me in accord with the measure of my faith. Grant me a boundless faith in You, such as You deserve.*

What comes out of the mouth originates in the mind.

JULY 16

—Mt 15:18

REFLECTION. Healthy water will never flow from a putrid well; and a heart full of carnal desires will never give rise to anything pure.

The causes of evil must first be removed and then the wicked effects will also disappear.

PRAYER. *Lord, create a pure heart within me. Let me live a holy life in Your presence.*

Give glory to the Lord, your God, before it grows dark. —Jer 13:16

JULY 17

REFLECTION. Nothing is lost when one is converted while there is still time. But if one lets the hour of conversion go by, the darkness of night will fall, when nobody can work. Then only judgment is left.

Do I want to reach such a point?

PRAYER. *Merciful God, be for me, one day, not a judge but my Savior!*

JULY 18

God himself has taught you to love one another. —1 Thes 4:9

REFLECTION. Only one way leads to the human heart: the way of love. God Himself has walked this way! Thus, the Cross becomes the school of love.

Those who learn everyday in this school will find the way to be united with their brothers and sisters in love.

PRAYER. *Most loving Jesus, let Your love make me loving and Your sacrifice make me ready to give myself to others.*

JULY 19

God makes all things work together for the good of those who have been called. —Rom 8:28

REFLECTION. Those who love God are drawn nearer to the Father by every circumstance of daily life—joy brings them closer by ties of loving gratitude, and sorrow by the painful way of the Cross.

Those who do not love God become haughty and forget Him in the passing joys of this life and in sadness become bitter and desperate.

PRAYER. *Lord, grant me Your true love. This is all I need.*

He called his servants and handed his funds over to them according to each man's abilities.

—Mt 25:14

JULY 20

REFLECTION. Nobody is exempt from rendering a final accounting. However, God does not judge us according to the quantity of our work but according to the measure of fidelity with which we have used the gifts given to us.

Do not envy others what has been given to them but work with what has been given to you.

PRAYER. *Good Father, do not judge me according to what I have done, but according to what I honestly strive to do.*

Do not worry about your livelihood.

—Mt 6:25

JULY 21

REFLECTION. People can become slaves not only of those things that they have, but also of those that they do not have. The anguish over the cares of this world makes people blind and insensible to what is higher and spiritual.

Those who serve God faithfully can trust in Him, even for the necessities of their life on earth.

PRAYER. *Heavenly Father, I give You thanks because I can be sure of Your help also for all that regards my body.*

JULY 22

The first requirement of an administrator is that he prove trustworthy. —1 Cor 4:2

REFLECTION. Being trustworthy in faith, trustworthy in prayer, and trustworthy in the struggle for sanctification—this is my daily task in life. One day I will be judged according to this trustworthiness, not according to earthly success or failure.

Have I always been trustworthy? What must I do now to become even more trustworthy?

PRAYER. *My Lord and my God, make me always Your good and trustworthy servant. Grant that I may partake of eternal joy.*

JULY 23

You shall love the Lord your God with your whole heart, with your whole soul, and with all your mind. —Mt 22:37

REFLECTION. God is jealous and does not want to share His love with anybody else. I must love Him without any "ifs" and without any "buts," without reserve and without conditions. Then He will give me also the gift of His boundless love.

PRAYER. *God of love, grant that I may be Yours with everything that I am and have. Free me from anything that takes me away from You.*

You must put on that new man created in God's image.
—Eph 4:24

JULY 24

REFLECTION. The new self created in God's image can be born in me only when the old self is dead. For this constant watchfulness and struggle is necessary.

The old self always returns and tries to prevail. What am I doing to root out that self?

PRAYER. *My Father, give me the understanding of Christ. Strengthen me to practice acts of mortification which will aid me in the constant struggle to attain to living a life in the fullness of Christ.*

Athletes deny themselves . . . to win a crown of leaves that withers, but we a crown that is imperishable.
—1 Cor 9:25

JULY 25

REFLECTION. Those who ambitiously desire worldly prizes are ready to sacrifice anything for them: their time, energies, rest, etc.

Is not our eternal destination at least just as worthy of our dedication of equal time and energy? Do I think of this during the day?

PRAYER. *My Lord and my Savior, forgive all my sinfulness. Help me to seek You with my whole being that I may happily accomplish the purpose of my earthly life.*

JULY 26

By your words you will be acquitted, and by your words you will be condemned. —Mt 12:37

REFLECTION. God will judge us not only according to everything we have done, but also according to everything we have said. Words have great power. A single word may become for us either a blessing or a curse! It can be the reason for a person's perdition.

Therefore, care is necessary in all our speech—even in every single word we say!

PRAYER. *Lord, create in me a pure heart, so that even the words I say may be pure and pleasing to You.*

JULY 27

By waiting and by calm you shall be saved. —Is 30:15

REFLECTION. The human heart needs silence. Silence makes us strong and receptive to the inspiration of the Holy Spirit.

We must be careful not to disturb the work of Divine grace by useless or uncharitable talk.

PRAYER. *Lord, in You I put all my trust. Help me to spend time in quiet reflection each day to listen to Your inspirations.*

If [the grain of wheat] dies, it produces much fruit. —Jn 12:24

JULY 28

REFLECTION. It is a natural law that what is inferior must be sacrificed for what is better. Lonely and fruitless is the life of the old self of sin.

Those who sacrifice this self and devote themselves to God in obedience rise with a new spiritual life. Their lives will be eternally fruitful.

PRAYER. *My Savior, help me to die with You, so that I may live with You for all eternity.*

Woe to that man through whom scandal comes. —Mt 18:7

JULY 29

REFLECTION. Our influence should help to improve our neighbors, not to scandalize them or harm their souls.

Christians, therefore, can never be too vigilant to insure that their life and conduct will not do harm to anyone!

PRAYER. *Heavenly Father, grant to me and to all human beings the grace necessary for salvation.*

JULY 30 *Tax collectors and prostitutes are entering the kingdom of God before you.* —Mt 21:31

REFLECTION. Repentant public sinners can obtain conversion and forgiveness more easily than those who have the false piety of the Pharisees and are wholly pleased with themselves.

Do not judge or throw the first stone at anyone who commits sin. Leave the judgment entirely to Almighty God.

PRAYER. *Heavenly Father, Your compassion is boundless. Be merciful to all those who are yearning for You.*

JULY 31 *Enter through the narrow gate.* —Mt 7:13

REFLECTION. Narrow is the gate that leads from this world into heaven. Only through sorrow, repentance, and victory over self will those who are haughty attain union with God.

Is not this end worthy of any sacrifice?

PRAYER. *God, You are my highest Good. No road will be too long if it leads me to You, no sacrifice too hard. Bless and strengthen my good will!*

A good man produces goodness from the good in his heart.

—Lk 6:45

AUG. 1

REFLECTION. The value of human beings is not based so much upon their deeds as upon their intentions. Hence, it is not enough to avoid evil deeds. It is necessary to aspire to attain a pure heart.

Do my actions radiate an inner righteousness?

PRAYER. *My Lord and Savior, I consecrate my heart to You. Stamp it with the seal of Your goodness so that only goodness may flow from it.*

No one who comes [to me] will I ever reject.

—Jn 6:37

AUG. 2

REFLECTION. These words should inspire faith and hope. Our Lord asks for nothing extraordinary—only that I go to Him. This means that I must choose Him above all else—that I must with a sincere and honest intention take the road which leads to Him.

Then, in His grace, He will welcome me— even if I should come to Him as a sinner, like the Prodigal Son.

PRAYER. *My Savior, how good You are! Do not be far from me, but grant that some day I may reach the happiness of my supernatural destiny.*

AUG. 3

Because of your faith it shall be done to you. —Mt 9:29

REFLECTION. God's love and power are boundless. But in order that they may work efficaciously they require that we have the faith of a child.

God always manifests His glory wherever He finds living faith—a faith that goes beyond the understanding of the human mind.

PRAYER. *Lord, I trust in You because You are all-powerful and never err.*

AUG. 4

Commit to the Lord your way; trust in him, and he will act. —Ps 37:5

REFLECTION. Try to make your way pleasing to God. He will then make everything work for your good. What He does may not necessarily be in accord with your ideas. But it will always be better than you could have hoped or deserved.

Is my way pleasing to God?

PRAYER. *Lord, guide me in everything. Grant that I may always follow the way of Your Divine will.*

Let them grow together until harvest.
—Mt 13:30

**AUG.
5**

REFLECTION. God's mercy is very often incomprehensible to us. Often in our eagerness we wish to anticipate God's judgment, but God's patience is for all eternity.

God keeps silent and waits. His judgment will give to each of us what we deserve.

PRAYER. *Good and just God, I obey You and Your laws. Have patience with me until I rest again in Your embrace.*

The Son of Man has come to search out and save what was lost.
—Lk 19:10

**AUG.
6**

REFLECTION. God seeks the souls who are in need and in danger just as a good shepherd seeks the lost sheep. How far away I must be from this loving and zealous God if I have no care for the return to the Father's house of all those who have gone astray! Sinners deserve help not scorn!

PRAYER. *Heavenly Father, grant to me and to all human beings the grace necessary for salvation.*

AUG. 7

Let the dead bury their dead.
—Lk 9:60

REFLECTION. When we are called by God to follow Him, there is only one thing to be done: obey Him immediately. Every other consideration must yield because it is an impediment to this obedience. It must be set aside at any cost, even if the price is our own life.

Do I consider the following of Christ all-important in my life?

PRAYER. *Lord, let me be prompt in accomplishing Your will totally and joyously, without hesitation of any kind.*

AUG. 8

We must undergo many trials if we are to enter the reign of God.
—Acts 14:22

REFLECTION. Our eternal destination is to enter the Kingdom of heaven. However, we must undergo many trials and tribulations to reach our goal, where we will have eternal happiness.

Are not all the sufferings that must be faced on the way worth our patient endurance in order to reach that destination—even if they include death?

PRAYER. *My Savior, strengthen me so that I may follow You. Let the cross of this world be one day my key to heaven.*

Never again shall anyone eat of your fruit. —Mk 11:14

**AUG.
9**

REFLECTION. Thus was cursed the fig tree which did not bear fruit. God's judgment is inexorable—even for human beings.

Woe to those who through a false hope in God's mercy let themselves be dissuaded from doing their duty faithfully.

PRAYER. *Lord, make me serve You always with perfect fidelity. Sanctify me and my way, so that one day I may be with You for all eternity.*

And who is my neighbor? —Lk 10:29

**AUG.
10**

REFLECTION. A disciple of Christ cannot ask: "Who is my neighbor?" He must ask: "Whose neighbor am I?" Who needs my help?

If someone is in need, I must seek to help him/her without asking any other question.

PRAYER. *Lord, be my Teacher. Give me open eyes and a compassionate heart toward the needs of others, that I may always fulfill Your commandment of love.*

AUG. 11

O Lord, great and mighty is your name.
—Jer 10:6

REFLECTION. God's almighty power is visible even today. If it is hidden from you it is because you are far away from God.

The closer you are to a mountain, the bigger it looks to you!

PRAYER. *Lord, make me recognize Your greatness and power so that this knowledge may benefit my life.*

AUG. 12

Comfort and upbuild one another as indeed you are doing.
—1 Thes 5:11

REFLECTION. It is the Christian's duty to help others to attain the Kingdom of God. This concerns the help that we must give to each other by prayer, an encouraging word, or a helping hand.

Do I do this, or am I an obstacle to anyone?

PRAYER. *Heavenly Father, may Your Reign be realized always more and more in me and also in all human beings—who are Your children.*

The harvest is good but laborers are scarce. —Mt 9:37 **AUG. 13**

REFLECTION. The plentiful harvest of God will necessarily be damaged if there are no people to gather it.

Have I myself not let pass precious moments to win souls for God? Have there not been times when God expected from me the fruits of His Divine grace in vain?

PRAYER. *Merciful God, forgive me all abuses of Your grace. Give me watchful eyes for the inspiration of Your Spirit, so that I may not hinder but foster its actions.*

Do not be afraid of those who kill the body and can do no more. —Lk 12:4 **AUG. 14**

REFLECTION. Those who are afraid of human beings will lapse into submission to them and will not serve God's Kingdom.

However, those who fear God above all else are truly wise and nothing can disturb them even if they should have to suffer and die.

PRAYER. *Lord, give me the strength to abandon all human fear and to serve You only.*

AUG.
15

Mary has chosen the better portion. —Lk 10:42

REFLECTION. To work for God is a good thing, but to devote oneself to His holy will is better. This is why Mary, Mother of God, chose the better part, because her whole life was dedicated to doing God's will.

Her assumption to heaven in body and soul was the crowning of this life totally given to God.

PRAYER. *Heavenly Father, let us follow the example of the Queen of Heaven. May we serve You through the most faithful accomplishment of Your holy will, and so reach our eternal destiny.*

AUG.
16

Grow rather in grace, and in the knowledge of our Lord and Savior Jesus Christ. —2 Pt 3:18

REFLECTION. Life supposes growth. When this growth is lacking, it leads to deterioration and death. In the same manner, our spiritual life can know no decline in growth.

If we stop growing spiritually, we begin to deteriorate and end up in spiritual ruin. At what point do I stand now?

PRAYER. *My God and Lord, let me grow from day to day in Your grace, and thus get nearer to You.*

Ask, and you will receive. Seek, and you will find. Knock, and it will be opened to you. —Mt 7:7

REFLECTION. This word is like a "gift" from God's treasure! It makes a magnificent promise to those who pray with a faith as solid as a rock, seek with filial humility, or knock with constant patience.

They will always experience that God keeps His word. For He is ever faithful.

PRAYER. *My God, I give You thanks with all my heart for Your promises. Grant that they may be fulfilled in me.*

I fast twice a week, I pay tithes on all I possess. —Lk 18:12

REFLECTION. The value of our acts is determined by the intention of our heart. If the intention is evil, all other external acts of piety are useless. But if the intention is right, then everything done is good and blessed.

PRAYER. *Lord, let me be good always, that I may become worthy of Your good pleasure!*

AUG. 19

Whoever loves father or mother more than me is not worthy of me.
—Mt 10:37

REFLECTION. Blood ties are holy and willed by God. However, those who let themselves be separated from God by these earthly ties distort that which is holy and willed by God and become sinners.

What are my relations with God? Is He my One and my All? Or do I permit some creature to be such?

PRAYER. *Lord, cleanse and sanctify my love. Grant that You alone may be the First and the Last in my life!*

AUG. 20

Teacher, does it not matter to you that we are going to drown?
—Mk 4:38

REFLECTION. How quickly our lack of faith is revealed when any obstacle rises in our path. Yet God has done nothing to deserve my mistrust!

God is always present and never acts too late, even when it seems that He is asleep. I must place more confidence in what He does and in His providence.

PRAYER. *Father, at Your feet I place all my fears. Let me trust in You in life and in death.*

The reign of God is like a mustard seed. **AUG.**
—Mt 13:31 **21**

REFLECTION. Never judge by appearances. The works of God have uneventful and barely discernible beginnings.

However, such beginnings give rise to a miracle for those who, with patience and perseverance, let God's work mature. Am I among those who do this?

PRAYER. *Eternal God, forgive me if I have been impatient. Give me all that I need to persevere until the end.*

My sheep hear my voice. I know them, and they follow me. **AUG.**
—Jn 10:27 **22**

REFLECTION. The Savior knows all His children in detail—with their individual talents, their limitations, their needs and necessities—and takes care of each of them with a shepherd's tenderness.

What He asks of us is simply to place our trust in Him and follow Him. Is the Lord not deserving of this?

PRAYER. *My Savior, bless me so that I may follow You in all paths.*

AUG. 23

Salt is good, but if salt loses its flavor what good is it for seasoning? —Lk 14:34

REFLECTION. It is the duty of Christians to put an end to the corruption of morals and the general depravity in the world.

Those who want to carry out this duty cannot adapt themselves to the corrupt habit of the world. They must be like salt that seasons the world for good.

PRAYER. *Lord, give me the fullness of Your Spirit. Help me to do only good in Your Kingdom.*

AUG. 24

Help carry one another's burdens; in that way you will fulfill the law of Christ. —Gal 6:2

REFLECTION. Every need of our neighbor is a call to our Christian duty. It summons us to demonstrate our love for others.

This love does not look only at our own sorrows. Filled with compassion, it helps us to bear the sorrows of others as well. Am I attentive to this call?

PRAYER. *My Father, let my greatest work be to love You and to show my love in loving deeds.*

Seek first his kingship over you . . . and all these things will be given to you besides.

AUG.
25

—Mt 6:33

REFLECTION. Worldly concerns rob us of much time, energy, and joy. Have more trust and let the Kingdom of God be your greatest interest.

If you do this, daily cares will disappear. The Father will take care of all your needs.

PRAYER. *Almighty and eternal God, let me seek always those things that are Yours. Help me in all my temporal and spiritual needs.*

He who calls us is trustworthy, therefore he will do it.

AUG.
26

—1 Thes 5:24

REFLECTION. God does not call us just to abandon us later to our own fates without any help. Since He cannot deny Himself, He cannot be unfaithful.

He gives not only a good beginning but also a good end. We have only to grasp His blessed hand.

PRAYER. *Heavenly Father, firm as a rock is Your trust among the waters of my infidelity and my weakness. You are my strength in life and in death.*

AUG. 27

Show me the way in which I should walk. —Ps 143:8

REFLECTION. To show the way to us is God's task. But to walk along this way is our task. And we cannot walk away from it.

What good is it for me to know the way if I do not follow it? Or if I abandon it before reaching my goal?

PRAYER. *My Lord and Master, make me all-holy. With faithful love, may I follow You in all Your ways.*

AUG. 28

If you find that the world hates you, know it has hated me before you. —Jn 15:18

REFLECTION. It is proper to the vocation of disciples of Christ to sow love and reap hatred. Do not be saddened by this.

Look upon the hatred shown you as a scale. The greater the weight of that hatred, the more authentic will be your love in bearing it.

PRAYER. *My Savior, bind me wholly to You and make me willing to suffer all things for You. Let me share in Your sufferings so that I may also share in Your everlasting glory.*

Everyone will be salted with fire. **AUG.**
—Mk 9:49
29

REFLECTION. All of us must control our own flesh and its wicked desires with the salt of serious discipline and self-denial. Otherwise we will become victims of our flesh.

Hence, I must avoid giving in to any evil inclinations.

PRAYER. *My Jesus, strengthen me in the battle against the old self. Let me grow more and more like You.*

Then go and do the same. **AUG.**
—Lk 10:37
30

REFLECTION. We do not need learned considerations about the will of God. What we need is a constant concern to do God's will.

God shows us His will every day and every hour—through the events and circumstances of our lives. Am I making efforts to do that will?

PRAYER. *Lord, You know my weaknesses and my faults. Give me the strength and piety to serve You with faithful love, even when this is difficult for me.*

AUG. 31 *Lord, when my brother wrongs me, how often must I forgive him?* —Mt 18:21

REFLECTION. This is the question of persons who do not possess Christ. This is why there is so much suffering in the world

Those who want to have Christ as their model must be compassionate and forgive without limit. For God's forgiveness is also boundless.

PRAYER. *My Lord and my God, how ashamed I am of my selfishness and worldly feelings. Grant that in Your compassionate love I may be found worthy of Your mercy in the future judgment.*

SEPT. 1 *Where two or three are gathered in my name, there am I in their midst.* —Mt 18:20

REFLECTION. Christ can be present only when we gather in His Name. This means in His love, and, consequently, in the love of our neighbor.

God is not present where the spirit of love is missing and our wills are opposed to His. The road before me is clear.

PRAYER. *Jesus, my brother, make us a holy community. Help us to grow in love for You and for one another.*

128

When you have been invited go and sit in the lowest place.
—Lk 14:10

SEPT.
2

REFLECTION. The human desire for the first place is completely external and has no importance. It is a matter of pride and selfishness. Those who find joy in God's service will be happy in any place assigned to them.

What is my attitude? Do I look for preference?

PRAYER. *Humble Savior, let me overcome all worldly ambitions and be ever more pleasing to You.*

He who is not with me is against me.
—Mt 12:30

SEPT.
3

REFLECTION. Either we are with God, wholly and openly, or we are against Him. There is no middle course ruled by indifference, laziness, and cowardice.

Christ offered Himself without reservation. Is He not worthy of all my devotion?

PRAYER. *Lord, do not let me be lukewarm. Help me to serve You with complete fidelity.*

SEPT. 4 *This man welcomes sinners and eats with them.* —Lk 15:2

REFLECTION. God rejects sin but not sinners. He seeks them out to free them from their misery.

All love should work thus: not condemning but helping even if it is only with a silent prayer. Do I pray for the conversion of souls?

PRAYER. *Most loving God, to Your grace I commend all persons, especially those who are far away from You. Have patience with us all and let us meet happily one day in Your eternal dwelling.*

SEPT. 5 *They that hope in the Lord will renew their strength.* —Is 40:31

REFLECTION. Those who do not want to succumb in the hard fight for life and eternity need their strength renewed each day. For God does not generally change the circumstances and the persons who are part of our life and who sometimes cause us suffering.

However, to those who trust in Him without reservation, God gives the strength they need. Do I trust in God even when He makes me wait for a long time?

PRAYER. *Lord God, forever faithful, restore and kindle my soul every day. Grant that I may run swiftly to meet You.*

130

Only with difficulty will a rich man enter into the kingdom of God.
—Mt 19:23

REFLECTION. Wealth is powerful and it opens many doors. But wealth is also powerless in the eyes of those whose hopes are fixed on external things—unless it is used in accord with God's plans, as a gift entrusted to us.

What do I prefer to be: poor in money and rich in grace—or the other way around?

PRAYER. *My Father, help me to be detached from earthly goods, so that I may better attain those of heaven.*

The reign of God is already in your midst.
—Lk 17:21

REFLECTION. The spirit of God reigns in His Kingdom. It is the spirit of love.

Do I have the same spirit of love that marks me also as a member of God's Kingdom?

PRAYER. *Eternal God, may Your Kingdom come also in me. Remove from my soul anything that may hinder Your Reign within me.*

SEPT. 8
The virgin shall be with child, and bear a son, and shall name him Immanuel. —Is 7:14

REFLECTION. The virginity of Mary is not only corporal but also spiritual. It means a total dedication to God, a consecration, a marriage with Him.

Love and veneration for her virginity are essential virtues of the true devotion to Mary. Unless we follow Mary by a total dedication to God's service, our lives will not be fruitful.

PRAYER. *Mary, most pure Mother, obtain for me the grace to dedicate my whole life, with all the strength of my body and soul, to serve God.*

SEPT. 9
Till your untilled ground, sow not among thorns. —Jer 4:3

REFLECTION. There is no rebirth, no renewal, without death to our selfishness. It is necessary to cultivate the entire heart; otherwise the thorns of sinful habits will always return to suffocate goodness.

Do I seek to do this? What am I doing to remove the impediments that until now have hindered the work of the Holy Spirit?

PRAYER. *Lord, my God, renew me and create in me a pure heart.*

The kingdom of God will be taken away from you and given to a nation that will yield a rich harvest.
—Mt 21:43

SEPT.
10

REFLECTION.   Why was the chosen people rejected and the Kingdom of God taken from it? Because the people did not follow the Divine call.

Those who do not heed God's call, and instead of serving Him seek only their own pleasure, betray the Kingdom of God and will be rejected. Am I always faithful in doing God's will for me?

PRAYER.   *Almighty God, let me consecrate my whole life, all my time, and all my strength to Your service. Grant that I may use temporal things only to allow me to reach eternal values.*

If I were trying to win man's approval, I would surely not be serving Christ.
—Gal 1:10

SEPT.
11

REFLECTION.   We should certainly try to love other human beings and seek to please them, but never at the expense of displeasing God.

The Lord has the first place. I am not permitted to take away time and strength from Him in order to please human beings.

PRAYER.   *My Father, I would willingly be displeasing to others and to the world if this should please You.*

SEPT. 12

And his mother said to him: "Son, why have you done this to us?"
—Lk 2:48

REFLECTION. Mary had to learn in a hard school that the will of the heavenly Father was above everything else, even above the rights and wishes of her Divine motherhood.

Am I faithful to God's will even though this sometimes brings suffering and heartache.

PRAYER. *Lord, make me willing and strong in following the example of the Mother of Your Son. Help me to seek only Your will in my actions and sufferings and try to fulfill it with my whole heart.*

SEPT. 13

Make friends for yourselves through your use of this world's goods.
—Lk 16:9

REFLECTION. It is neither possible nor necessary to renounce all worldly goods. However, we must not use them merely for our pleasure.

We must use them for the cause of God. Then our use of the temporal goods of this world will acquire eternal value.

PRAYER. *My faithful Lord and my God, give me wise discernment. Let me rise above all earthly goods and concerns and never forget the one thing necessary.*

May I never boast of anything but the cross of our Lord Jesus Christ!
—Gal 6:14

SEPT.
14

REFLECTION. Since the moment when by His Death Christ redeemed mankind from eternal death, the Cross has become a symbol of honor.

Therefore, place all your strength in becoming a disciple of the Crucified Lord and find true happiness in the grace it brings.

PRAYER. *My Savior, You do not give the Cross without grace, nor grace without the Cross. Let me understand the meaning of the Cross so that I may partake of its blessings.*

The apostles said to the Lord: "Increase our faith."
—Lk 17:5

SEPT.
15

REFLECTION. God does not impose upon you more than you can bear. No matter how great the anguish, heavy the oppression, and dark the future, retain a solid faith in God.

Such a faith will always sustain you. It will provide the strength you need to bear the burdens of life.

PRAYER. *Heavenly Father, increase my faith.*

SEPT. 16 *In your prayer do not rattle on like the pagans ... by the sheer multiplication of words.* —Mt 6:7

REFLECTION. Prayers are not measured by their length or their outward marks of devotion. Human words alone have no value.

True prayer comes from the heart through faith. Why do I pay so little attention to this in my prayers?

PRAYER. *Lord, teach me how to pray. Let me come to You as children come to their father.*

SEPT. 17 *A little yeast can affect the entire dough.* —Gal 5:9

REFLECTION. Little causes ... great results! This is true not only of evil but also of good.

Therefore, heed the good things even in the most humble forms, and beware of evil in its most insignificant beginnings.

PRAYER. *Almighty and eternal God, make me faithful even in the smallest things. Never let me forget that I must answer for everything before You.*

When a man knows the right thing to do and does not do it, he sins. **SEPT.** —Jas 4:17 **18**

REFLECTION. We sin not only by the evil we do in thoughts, words, and actions, but also by the good we fail to do—the opportunities for doing good that we allow to pass us by.

Do I examine my conscience also with respect to sins of omission?

PRAYER. *Lord, help me always to do good. Let me be a blessing for my brothers and sisters.*

―――――――――

None of you can be my disciple if he does not renounce all his possessions. **SEPT.** —Lk 14:33 **19**

REFLECTION. True disciples do not tolerate mediocrity. Those who do not wish to renounce earthly goods and pleasures have dedicated themselves to God. Saying "yes" to God entails saying "no" to the world.

If I can find everything in God, why do I fail to utter my "yes" to Him?

PRAYER. *My Savior, to become Your disciple is the greatest happiness. Never let me lose this happiness through my own infidelity.*

SEPT. 20

If a man is true to my word he shall never see death. —Jn 8:51

REFLECTION. Death should not be like a dreaded specter at the end of our life, but like a friend who opens the doors to eternal glory for us. The only condition required by our Savior is to keep His word and commandments.

If I willingly obey this, I will not have to fear death.

PRAYER. *Lord, grant that after this earthly life I may one day return in joy to my heavenly home.*

———————

SEPT. 21

What profit would a man show if he were to gain the whole world and destroy himself in the process? —Mt 16:26

REFLECTION. Human work and the acquisition of earthly goods are necessary to preserve our lives. However, if the interior life of the soul is damaged in the process, such a loss cannot be compensated for even by the whole world with all its wealth and values.

Therefore, we must pay attention to the one thing necessary.

PRAYER. *Lord, teach me to avoid any gain that does harm to me. Help me to welcome any loss that fosters the growth of my spiritual life*

Love never fails. —1 Cor 13:8

SEPT.
22

REFLECTION. God is love. God is eternal. Therefore, His love is also everlasting.

The sun of His love is always in heaven even when you, because of dark clouds, cannot see it.

PRAYER. *My Father, I give You thanks for the inexhaustible fount of Your love. Never stop loving me, even though Your love is shown in the symbol of the Cross.*

I am in your midst as the one who serves you. —Lk 22:27

SEPT.
23

REFLECTION. How foolish is the world's opinion that regards service as humiliating! It is not service that is degrading—but sin. To serve is an honor, for Christ Himself came among us to serve.

This service must be one of self-denial, humility, and love. Then it will be true service according to the example of our Savior and it will obtain God's reward.

PRAYER. *Loving Savior, You became the servant of us all. Let me serve You always in my brothers and sisters.*

SEPT. 24

Through Jesus Christ may he carry out in you all that is pleasing to him.
—Heb 13:21

REFLECTION. We must bear witness to the Lord's redemption—but we must do so through our conduct rather than our fine words.

To do God's will, to walk according to His word, to live in His grace, and to die in His peace—this is the best way to show that even today the Lord is alive, and powerful.

PRAYER. *Lord of life, let Your grace be always efficacious in me, and make me Your instrument in bringing it to others.*

SEPT. 25

The reign of God is like a buried treasure which a man found in a field.
—Mt 13:44

REFLECTION. God does not argue: He demands a total dedication. He wants us to pay something in order to obtain that wonderful treasure of being members of His Kingdom.

What sacrifice do I make for this purpose?

PRAYER. *Infinite God, loving Father, You are mine and I want to be Yours. Let me joyfully sacrifice anything that hinders me from enjoying the magnificence of Your Kingdom.*

A second time he put his question: "Simon, son of John, do you love me?" —Jn 21:16

SEPT. 26

REFLECTION. This question is directed also to me. And my eternal destiny will hinge on how I answer it.

Can I speak of love if I do not show it with actions?

PRAYER. *Sacred Heart of Jesus, let me love You ever more and more!*

God is the Lord to one who waits for him, to the soul that seeks him. —Lam 3:25

SEPT. 27

REFLECTION. It is a fundamental law of faith and experience that God takes care of us if we have concern for His interests. Then do not complain of God by saying that He is not good to you.

Rather strike your breast in sorrow. For you have often turned your back on Him by your sins.

PRAYER. *Lord, forgive all my ingratitude and unfaithfulness. Give me an unquenchable desire for You. Make me bear in my heart and seek no one else but You, Father of all goodness.*

141

SEPT. 28

If anyone thirsts, let him come to me. —Jn 7:37

REFLECTION. To those who are satisfied the Lord has nothing to say. But those who thirst for Him, who desire Him, He will not reject.

This is true even when they have to come from the far-away places where sin has led them.

PRAYER. *My Savior, refresh my thirsty soul with the waters of Your grace and Your love. Let me be sated and healed.*

SEPT. 29

Wake up, and strengthen what remains before it dies. —Rv 3:2

REFLECTION. It is not enough to think and act only for self and to act for one's own soul and eternity.

Those who are blessed must also be a blessing for their brothers and sisters and seek to bring them to God.

PRAYER. *Most loving Father, strengthen my weakness by Your grace. Make use of me as a faithful helper in Your Kingdom.*

If . . . by the spirit you put to death the evil deeds of the body, you will live. —Rom 6:13

SEPT. 30

REFLECTION. No mediocrity is permitted or possible with God. Either we discipline the flesh, which is our own body, or its demands will rule us.

What am I determined to do—to discipline the flesh or to be ruled by it?

PRAYER. *Lord, how many times I have gone against the inspirations of the Holy Spirit within me! Grant that in the future I may always follow His voice rather than my own inclinations, so that one day I may be united with You.*

It is I. Do not be afraid! —Mt 14:27

OCT. 1

REFLECTION. In everything that happens to me I can hear the comforting words: "It is I. Do not be afraid!" God is with me in every trouble.

This should inspire a boundless trust in me. Let me cast out all fear for I have God's boundless love, and with Him I have everything.

PRAYER. *Lord, be in me and stay with me in life and death.*

OCT. 2 *If possible, live peaceably with everyone.* —Rom 12:18

REFLECTION. How happy we would be if we could live in peace with all human beings! But this is not possible.

If friendship for the world turns us into enemies of God, Christians must necessarily resist. This is a condition for peace with God.

PRAYER. *Eternal God, let me be always an ambassador of Your peace. Grant that all human beings may seek and find peace.*

OCT. 3 *Let anyone who thinks he is standing upright watch out lest he fall!* —1 Cor 10:12

REFLECTION. Self-confidence is necessary, but when it becomes self-aggrandizement it is dangerous. Nothing leads more easily to ruin than pride in one's own power. And nothing protects more efficiently from ruin than humility.

Humility enables us to pray for God's help and protection in all things.

PRAYER. *Almighty Father, give me Your blessed hand. Let nothing separate me from You.*

This man was with Jesus the **OCT.**
Nazorean. —Mt 26:71 **4**

REFLECTION. This would be a wonderful epigraph and a wonderful judgment by God. But woe to me if already in my lifetime it can be said: once he was with Jesus . . . but not now.

Yes, today it is difficult to live with Jesus. But it is more difficult to live without Him and incomparably more difficult to die without Him.

PRAYER. *My Savior and Redeemer, let me be Your faithful disciple forever.*

Whoever puts his hand to the **OCT.**
plow but keeps looking back is **5**
unfit for the reign of God.
—Lk 9:62

REFLECTION. An irregular furrow is made by the person who, when plowing the land, turns to look back. Likewise, the person who judges according to the world loses sight of the radiant goal of the Kingdom of God.

Those who want to serve God must burn their bridges behind them and be completely at His disposal. Am I ready for this?

PRAYER. *Lord and Savior, You have called me. Keep me steadfast in all Your ways until the end.*

145

OCT. 6

Clearly you are a letter from Christ. —2 Cor 3:3

REFLECTION. To be a letter—that is, a revelation from God—what a great vocation! If only others could read in our lives as in the Sacred Scriptures! If only all Christians could be a living, convincing sermon of the Lord! If only each of us could shine as a sun of divine love, able to be read even by those who do not know God's written word!

What do others read in me? What spirit guides my actions?

PRAYER. *My Jesus, make me imitate You. Let me be a blessing for others.*

OCT. 7

The greatest among you will be the one who serves the rest. —Mt 23:11

REFLECTION. "To be the one who serves" means to face every day the sacrifices required by charity. It means to forget oneself and to live for others. It means to forgo our rights and be concerned only with our duties.

Do I strive to acquire this spirit of disinterested service? Only on this condition will I deserve the name of "Christian."

PRAYER. *Most loving Savior, You want me to serve You in others. Make me willing and ready to do it with Your grace.*

Do not be surprised, beloved, that a trial by fire is occurring in your midst. —1 Pt 4:12

OCT. 8

REFLECTION. No seed bears fruit without the sun. In the same way, our inner self will never grow without the fire of suffering.

Hence, do not complain about the cross God has given you. Rather thank Him for working in you and being concerned about you.

PRAYER. *Faithful God, give me strength to accept my sufferings. Let them bear fruit in my life.*

How blest are the poor in spirit; the reign of God is theirs. —Mt 5:3

OCT. 9

REFLECTION. The Kingdom of God begins in this life already, and so does His happiness. Blest are they who are detached from earthly goods in their inner selves.

They are truly poor because they are such in God's eyes and because they are on the way to God. Only those who are poor in spirit can be enriched and blessed by God.

PRAYER. *Lord, make me poor in myself and rich in You. Then I will have no desires apart from You and will experience true happiness.*

OCT. 10

Blest are the sorrowing; they shall be consoled. —Mt 5:4

REFLECTION. The Cross is a grace and a blessing. It is like a sacred fountain in which human beings are cleansed by a kind of baptism. They are born again, mature and are enriched with new strength.

Therefore, think not only of the burden of the Cross, but also of its blessings.

PRAYER. *Most loving Father, comfort me when I need it and give me strength when You see me suffering. Let me never avoid the Cross and its blessings.*

OCT. 11

Blest are the lowly, they shall inherit the land. —Mt 5:5

REFLECTION. Those who are selfish and without scruples make a career in the world; the lowly are set aside.

However, experience teaches that the opportunists will not conquer the world, but the lowly will conquer hearts.

PRAYER. *Jesus, my model, I want to be the same way You were: lowly and humble of heart. Help me to fight the good fight against my own nature so that the promised blessing may descend upon me.*

148

Blest are they who hunger and thirst for holiness; they shall have their fill. —Mt 5:6

REFLECTION. Those who hunger and thirst for holiness and for the Kingdom of God are aware of their own lowliness. They extend their hands toward the hands of Christ the Redeemer and draw abundantly from the fountain of divine grace.

On the other hand, those who have a self-satisfied virtue and a comfortable piety will find themselves before a closed door.

PRAYER. *Heavenly Father, make me grow each day in goodness. Let me seek rather to become better than to have the best.*

Blest are they who show mercy; mercy shall be theirs. —Mt 5:7

REFLECTION. The needs of others should be our own needs. The barriers of sin and the stumbling stones of human ingratitude which lie in the way must be overcome by our mercy.

In this way, we too will be assured of God's mercy.

PRAYER. *God of goodness, enlarge my heart with Your merciful love. Let the miracle of Your mercy shine through me for Your honor and glory.*

OCT. 14

Blest are the single-hearted, for they shall see God. —Mt 5:8

REFLECTION. A divided or impure heart can ruin a whole life. This intimate source of our thoughts, sensations, and feelings should be pure, that is, without blemish like refined gold.

Only then can we see the truth, beauty, and love of God and be capable of embracing Him, understanding Him, and seeing Him as He is.

PRAYER. *Lord, create a pure heart in me.*

OCT. 15

Blest too the peace-makers; they shall be called sons of God. —Mt 5:9

REFLECTION. Those who want to dedicate themselves to the service of peace must overcome the barriers created by hatred, envy, and selfishness. To do so they must have within themselves the peace of the Holy Spirit. There can be no peace in the world without peace with God.

What a sublime mission for the children of God!

PRAYER. *God of peace, sanctify all human beings. Bless their steps, that they may be messengers of Your peace.*

Blest are those persecuted for holiness' sake; the reign of God is theirs.
— Mt 5:10

OCT.
16

REFLECTION. Are you a true disciple of Christ? Then you will be despised and persecuted as was the Messiah before you. A Christianity that gives in to this world is not Christianity at all.

Thus, the hatred of this world is proof that your beliefs are opposed to the spirit of the world. You can take comfort in this.

PRAYER. *Most loving Savior, fill me with Your Spirit. Let me become ever more like You, even though the world rejects me for this.*

Never cease praying.
— 1 Thes 5:17

OCT.
17

REFLECTION. If one prays little the reason behind this habit is not lack of time, but lack of love. A man who prays is blessed. Everything that happens, whether it makes him glad or makes him suffer, becomes for him a way that leads to happiness with God.

How often do I pray? Only when in need, or frequently?

PRAYER. *Lord, teach me how to pray. Grant that I may be happy in being with You.*

151

OCT. 18

You need patience to do God's will and receive what he has promised. —Heb 10:36

REFLECTION. Impatience is weakness, stubbornness, and does not follow God's way. On the other hand, patience is a force that does God's will.

Patience is a living faith expressed in daily deeds and confirmed by suffering. It adheres to God and hence is assured of His Divine promises.

PRAYER. *Most loving Father, strengthen my trust in You. Help me to bear patiently everything that Your holy will asks of me.*

OCT. 19

If you can interpret the portents of earth and sky, why can you not interpret the present time? —Lk 12:56

REFLECTION. Do not be like worldly persons. They see only what happens in the visible world of the senses.

Incomparably more important is the truth of the invisible world. But it is hidden behind the veil of visible reality.

PRAYER. *Almighty God, help me to look at temporal events through the prism of eternity. Let them thus bear fruits for my soul.*

Because you are lukewarm ... I will spew you out of my mouth!
—Rv 3:15-16

REFLECTION. Tepidity is the worst thing in the sight of God. It is better to be cold than lukewarm.

From a Saul, a Paul was born. But from an indifferent soul like Pilate's, no Christian has ever been born.

PRAYER. *Heavenly Father, protect me against lukewarmness. Bless me so that I may serve You always with ardent zeal and so grow ever closer to You.*

I will break away and return to my father.
—Lk 15:18

REFLECTION. Sin is separation from God and deviation from the right path. We must "break away" from this path of sin if we want to return to our Father's house.

Prayer alone is not enough. We must be wholly converted to God in all our thoughts, words, and actions as well.

PRAYER. *Father, I give You thanks because I can come back to You always, even when I have strayed far away from You. Keep me firm and do not let me walk again in the path of sin.*

OCT. 22

No prophet is without honor except in his native place.
—Mk 6:4

REFLECTION. Those who do not accept the truth do not accept the testimony of the truth either. They go looking for its defects in order to justify their rejection of it with their conscience.

Therefore, always be careful to bear witness to God through a life that is blameless.

PRAYER. *God of goodness, make my way always pure and holy. Let no one who is weak be scandalized because of me.*

OCT. 23

Every planting not put down by my heavenly Father will be uprooted.
—Mt 15:13

REFLECTION. We see here a very pious weed overlaid with what looks like greenery and apparently bearing plentiful fruit. But it will be uprooted.

Genuine spiritual life exists only when the roots are secured in the Divine life, in grace, and in love.

PRAYER. *Lord God, You are the Creator of life. Grant that I may live for You, in You, and by You, that I may be worthy of eternal life.*

We are useless servants. We have done no more than our duty.

—Lk 17:10

OCT. 24

REFLECTION. Anything good that you do is only your duty and grace. Do not be proud of your deeds and do not think of what you have done, but of what you have not done.

Then you will remain humble in spite of any successes that may come to you. Only in this manner will you be pleasing to God.

PRAYER. *Infinitely good God, I do not have any claims to Your grace. Let it be Your gift to me for the sake of Your Son.*

The Lord will complete what he has done for me; your kindness, O Lord, endures forever.

—Ps 138:8

OCT. 25

REFLECTION. God completes His work of grace in all those who do not separate themselves from His fatherly care, because His kindness endures forever.

Can there be a greater assurance of faith and certainty of salvation for me than this?

PRAYER. *Lord Jesus Christ Crucified, I commend myself in life and in death to Your blessed hands nailed to the Cross.*

OCT. 26

A bruised reed he shall not break, and a smoldering wick he shall not quench. —Is 42:3

REFLECTION. Jesus, fill with love and mercy, You are the last hope and comfort of those who are going to die and be destroyed. Even if the whole world should abandon, judge, and condemn me, You will never do so.

It is good for me if at least a glimmer of repentance and desire for God still burn within me.

PRAYER. *My Lord and God, I trust only in You. Bless and increase my faith.*

OCT. 27

I was speechless and opened not my mouth, because it was your doing. —Ps 39:10

REFLECTION. A time for silence is necessary. God drops His anchor only in still waters. When I speak, the Lord is silent; but when I am silent, He speaks to me and comforts my soul.

Should I not at least try this approach? It will assuredly be worthwhile.

PRAYER. *Lord, let me be silent before You when You speak to me and wish to work in me.*

156

Faith is confident assurance concerning what we hope for, and conviction about things we do not see. —Heb 11:1

OCT. 28

REFLECTION. Faith should make us happy and strong, faithful and secure because God's authority stands behind it! It becomes a living force that cannot be imagined.

Do I strive to preserve and increase this faith?

PRAYER. *Heavenly Father, I am happy to be able to deposit all my trust in You. Strengthen my faith and do not let anything shake it.*

While everyone was asleep, his enemy came and sowed weeds through his wheat. —Mt 13:25

OCT. 29

REFLECTION. Why do you complain of the weeds in the field of God? Rather, strike your breast.

You too are guilty of contributing to this through your torpor, indifference, and negligence.

PRAYER. *My God and Father, forgive all my negligence and unfaithfulness. Bless me and all creatures, so that one day You may accept us as good grain in Your granaries.*

OCT. 30

Your Father knows what you need before you ask him. —Mt 6:8

REFLECTION. Is not God my Father? Then of course I can tell Him all my hopes and worries, big or small, with filial trust and the assurance of being heard.

I have no need of many words. My all-knowing and loving Father will always give me what is necessary for my temporal and spiritual life.

PRAYER. *Heavenly Father, let me always walk before You in holiness. Then I will truly deserve Your love and Your help.*

———————

OCT. 31

The Son of Man has come to search out and save what was lost. —Lk 19:10

REFLECTION. Do not be deluded into thinking that you are authorized, or, what is worse, obliged, to judge others. True love follows Christ's example which does not seek to judge, but to save.

What am I doing to save others?

PRAYER. *Eternal God, You have boundless mercy and patience. Infuse these sentiments into my heart that I may bear fruits of mercy and peace.*

God tried them and found them worthy of himself. —Wis 3:5

NOV. 1

REFLECTION. How has God tried His Saints? By the virtue that is part of His own nature—by love. Those who remain faithful to love—even under the cross—and show their love by works of love are they who are worthy of God.

How would I stand up under God's trial?

PRAYER. *Heart of Jesus, burning with love for me, inflame my heart with love for You.*

We have [an eternal] dwelling provided for us by God. —2 Cor 5:1

NOV. 2

REFLECTION. All earthly suffering is transfigured in the hope of eternity. One day, when this difficult—and at times almost unbearable—life has passed, we will go to a magnificent eternal dwelling.

It has been prepared for us and will be ours provided that we have not renounced our heavenly citizenship.

PRAYER. *Perfect Father in heaven, let me always serve You faithfully. Grant that I may one day attain a happy return to You.*

NOV. 3 *Try to come in through the narrow door.* —Lk 13:23

REFLECTION. There is no need for subtle arguments concerning God's will and our eternal destiny.

Those who pass through the narrow door of self-denial and obedience to the will of God accomplish the works of salvation. These will attain eternal salvation.

PRAYER. *Just God, be always the luminous goal of my desires and my life. Let me one day attain my eternal dwelling with You.*

NOV. 4 *Draw close to God and he will draw close to you.* —Jas 4:8

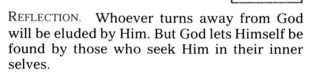

REFLECTION. Whoever turns away from God will be eluded by Him. But God lets Himself be found by those who seek Him in their inner selves.

Am I always aware of the presence of God? Or have I rejected Him through laziness and mediocrity, choosing my own path?

PRAYER. *Draw me ever closer to You, my God.*

No servant can serve two masters.
—Lk 16:13

NOV.
5

REFLECTION. God rejects mediocrity. He is a jealous God and wants to take complete possession of me.

That is why those who want to serve Him must do so with complete dedication. Is this my attitude in trying to serve God?

PRAYER. *My God and my All, I wish to belong to You in body and soul. Let me serve You always with total fidelity, so that my actions may find favor in Your sight.*

If you love those who love you, what merit is there in that?
—Mt 5:46

NOV.
6

REFLECTION. What we call love has its roots mostly in our own self and, therefore, is nothing else than selfish desire. But God demands a disinterested love that does not seek its own interests.

Only spiritual love can overcome the power of human wickedness.

PRAYER. *Good Father, Your Son shows Himself to both the just and the wicked. Let me resemble You in goodness and grant that through love I may conquer my enemies for You.*

161

NOV. 7 *God is Spirit, and those who worship him must worship in Spirit and truth.* —Jn 4:24

REFLECTION. Those who want to worship God in truth must give Him the honor that is His due.

God must be loved always and above all— even in work and among others—with simplicity, humility, sincerity, and purity of heart.

PRAYER. *Lord and God, let me lead a true spiritual life in total dedication to Your holy will so that I may worship You in Spirit and truth.*

NOV. 8 *Jesus started to indicate . . . that he must go to Jerusalem and suffer greatly.* —Mt 16:21

REFLECTION. Suffering is a school of life. Only through sufferings can human beings acquire the necessary capacity to be forbearing and the strength to attain inner growth. This is why God cannot take sufferings away from anyone.

I must trust Him and place my whole life under His guidance

PRAYER. *Lord, You cannot take the way of the Cross from anyone who wishes to come to You. Grant me a better understanding of this way and let me walk in it forever.*

Avoid greed in all its forms. **NOV.**
—Lk 12:15
9

REFLECTION. The greed for earthly goods enslaves and brings unhappiness to human beings!

Only those who possess God are happy—whether they have plenty or little!

PRAYER. *Lord, my greatest good, let me despise anything that does not lead me to You. Be the life and desire of my soul and make me happy in possessing You.*

Father. . . . —Mt 6:9 **NOV.**
10

REFLECTION. Christ's Redemption has given us a wonderful happiness: we have become children of God and partake of His Divine nature. In this way we have, at all moments, the right to the Father's love and care. But the Father also has the right to the love and obedience of His children.

Do I take this commitment seriously?

PRAYER. *Father, let me be always Your child in whom You can be pleased.*

NOV.
11 *Our Father. . . .* —Mt 6:9

REFLECTION. The community spirit is a duty of life. But a true, living community can be attained only when a sincere and disinterested love reigns. Among sisters and brothers of the same Father any selfishness, scorn, or prejudice must be excluded.

Do I regard all creatures as my brothers and sisters?

PRAYER. *Heavenly Father, let all human beings be Your dear children and my brothers and sisters.*

NOV.
12 *. . . in heaven.* —Mt 6:9

REFLECTION. This means that we are citizens not only of this earthly world, but also of another higher world. Our true homeland is heaven, to which we are destined to return.

This world is a preparation, a starting point that leads us to the Father Who is in heaven.

PRAYER. *My Father, let me live in such a way in this world of time that I may build my eternity.*

. . hallowed be your name.
—Mt 6:9

NOV.
13

REFLECTION. The salvation of the world is obtained through sanctification, that is, the glorification of the Divine Name in word and deed. This is God's will.

Are my life, my desires, my prayers, my actions, and my sufferings a constant hymn of burning love to the glorification of God's Name?

PRAYER. *Perfect Father, do not let me become lost among the earthly reflections of Your splendor. May You alone be my God and my All!*

Your kingdom come. —Mt 6:10

NOV.
14

REFLECTION. The Kingdom of God, insofar as it is a Kingdom of grace, has already come. What a great gift but at the same time what a grave responsibility! We must be ever more touched and moved by this grace in the depths of our beings.

We must always try to prepare the way for grace in our lives so that it may reform and renew us and the face of the earth.

PRAYER. *Lord, let me be a living stone in the building of Your Kingdom.*

NOV. 15

Your will be done on earth as it is in heaven.
—Mt 6:10

REFLECTION. Our salvation in time and in eternity depends entirely on how we conform our lives to God's will, accepting it with full generosity and fidelity of heart.

What is my attitude toward God's will? Do I see it and follow it in all that happens to me?

PRAYER. *Heavenly Father, let me always utter a resolute "Yes" whenever Your will calls me. Make me ready for any sacrifice.*

NOV. 16

Give us today our daily bread.
—Mt 6:11

REFLECTION. Concern for our daily bread should not be overestimated but neither should it be ignored.

Only in this way will we be able to give to the soul what is its due and to the body what is its due.

PRAYER. *Heavenly Father, give me and my brothers and sisters whatever is necessary for our daily earthly life. Enable us thus to fulfill in a better way the mission entrusted to us.*

And forgive us the wrong we have done as we forgive those who wrong us.
—Mt 6:12

NOV. 17

REFLECTION. Any sin, even the greatest, can be forgiven because God's mercy is infinitely greater than the sins of human beings. But God asks that we must also use mercy toward others, and see in every enemy an instrument of God.

Am I charitable and forgiving of the sins and faults of others?

PRAYER. *Lord, give me the strength and the grace to forgive all those who have wronged me. And let me in turn receive mercy from You.*

Subject us not to the trial.
—Mt 6:12

NOV. 18

REFLECTION. God permits temptations and trials not to make us fall, but to show forth our virtue and perseverance.

We must give proof of our strength; we must demonstrate that we oppose the allurements of evil and persevere constantly and without hesitation in the right path.

PRAYER. *Lord, help me to be watchful so that I may overcome all temptations. Help me in the struggle, so that I may conquer them and thus grow in Your grace.*

NOV. 19 *... but deliver us from the evil one.* —Mt 6:13

REFLECTION. The Evil One is constantly working to induce us to commit sin. To do so, he makes use of everything that leads to sin. But the redeeming grace of Christ frees us from the Evil One.

Do I seriously try to obtain this grace? Do I persevere in it in accord with my strength?

PRAYER. *Heavenly Father, You know what is dangerous for me. May Your grace guide me safely through this life and make me join You in heaven.*

NOV. 20 *"And you," he said to them, "who do you say that I am?"* —Mt 16:15

REFLECTION. We know and believe that the Christ is the Son of God. But is this faith strong enough to walk with Him even in the way of the Cross?

All faith which is not transformed into a total and personal dedication to Christ is dead.

PRAYER. *Jesus, Son of the living God, I believe in You, I hope in You, I love You. Let me be faithful to You unto death.*

If you live in me . . . ask what you will—it will be done. —Jn 15:7

NOV.
21

REFLECTION. Those who live in Jesus, who think His thoughts and are guided by His word, are "spiritual" persons. They desire only what Jesus wills.

Hence, their prayers will be heard. For they pray always in accord with God's will.

PRAYER. *Heavenly Father, I give You thanks because You give me everything I need for my spiritual and bodily life.*

Whoever does the will of God is brother and sister and mother to me. —Mk 3:35

NOV.
22

REFLECTION. To do God's will means to listen to His word and follow it. This gives rise to a communion of faith that is mysteriously regenerated by the Holy Spirit.

This communion of faith is incomparably better than any ties of blood. Have I experienced this renewal in me?

PRAYER. *Jesus, my brother, let my whole being be consumed in the will of the Father so that I may be worthy of Your love.*

NOV. 23

Whoever welcomes one such child for my sake welcomes me.

—Mt 18:3

REFLECTION. Everyone you meet is a messenger from God. Hence, do not pay attention to the rank or degree of people but look upon them as children of God

Welcome all those who come to you in the Name of Jesus—even if they are but children.

PRAYER. *Jesus, Son of God, You are brother to all human beings. Let me see and respect You in all without exception.*

NOV. 24

Do this and you shall live.

—Lk 10:28

REFLECTION. It is not what human beings do that brings about their salvation but what God does. Yet Christ requires the action of human beings as a condition of salvation.

What action does He require? The action of obeying God's will.

PRAYER. *My Savior, the will of the Father was the support of Your life. Give me also the strength to accomplish it, so that the doctrine of true faith may also become a life of faith.*

170

By faith Rahab the harlot escaped from being destroyed with the unbelievers. —Heb 11:31

NOV. 25

REFLECTION. The salvation of a harlot is a message of gladness. It also imparts hope to those who are lost without hope.

And what is the way to salvation? The faith that opens the heart to God's grace.

PRAYER. *Eternal Father, I believe in Your mercy and goodness. For the sake of this faith be merciful to me.*

Prepare the way for the people; . . . clear it of stones. —Is 62:10

NOV. 26

REFLECTION. How many stumbling stones are lying in the way: the stones of indifference, insensitivity, presumption, and hardness of heart! And many are hurt by them.

Do I try to remove them from my own path and the path of others? Do I try to bring all people I meet closer to God?

PRAYER. *My Father, do not let me be an obstacle for anyone. Make me the means to lead others closer to You.*

171

NOV. 27

More will be asked of a man to whom more has been entrusted.

—Lk 12:48

REFLECTION. Do not envy the gifts given to anyone. Be humble and content with what you have received.

God does not ask from individuals more than they can give. He is not concerned with quantity but with fidelity.

PRAYER. *Faithful God, You never ask too much from me. Strengthen my weakness and do not take into consideration what I have done but what I have wished to do.*

NOV. 28

I have left an open door before you which no one can close.

—Rv 3:8

REFLECTION. The door is open—free access to God's grace is open to all. No power on earth and no evil power of hell can close this door if I myself do not close it.

This is a grave responsibility for all human beings and for me: never to neglect grace, nor to put salvation in peril. Do I take this matter seriously?

PRAYER. *My Father, You accept all those who aspire to You. Never let me be separated from You.*

REFLECTION. Great is John the Baptist, but a child of God is even greater than he. Worldly pomp and wisdom disappear before the splendor of a redeemed soul.

This fact should make me happy—in spite of all sufferings.

PRAYER. *Heavenly Father, I give You thanks for the grace of Your Divine filiation. Let my behavior always correspond to this grace.*

REFLECTION. Earthly life is merely the time for sowing. Only at the Final Judgment will the harvest be gathered, the definitive separation of good from evil, of the grain from the chaff.

Those who do not serve the Kingdom of God and do not bear fruit for eternal life are the chaff and, as such, will be rejected. To which do I belong?

PRAYER. *Lord, take me in Your hands. Strengthen and protect me, and grant that one day I may bear precious fruit.*

DEC.
1

Your deliverance is near at hand.
—Lk 21:28

REFLECTION. "Deliverance" means Redemption—the joyful message of Advent! But I must go to meet my Redeemer with a pure heart and with a love ready for sacrifice.

If I do not do so, the Redemption cannot work effectively in me.

PRAYER. *My Savior, grant me Your spirit and Your way of thinking. Let me be ready for Christmas, for Your Divine birth in my soul.*

DEC.
2

The reign of God is at hand!
—Mt 1:15

REFLECTION. The coming of the Kingdom (or Reign) of God is the great mission of my life. It is in this world, but it is not of this world.

Therefore, I must eliminate the spirit of the world in my daily struggles if I am to become worthy of the Kingdom of God.

PRAYER. *Heavenly Father, free me, together with my fellow human beings, from the powers of darkness. Lead us all into the Kingdom of Your beloved Son.*

Reform your lives and believe in the gospel! —Mk 1:15

DEC. 3

REFLECTION. Penance does not only consist in external actions of mortification. It also involves an internal renewal, a conversion of soul.

I must become different and better interiorly, if the Gospel is to bear fruit in me.

PRAYER. *Holy Spirit, enlighten me and give me a change of heart. Move me to produce worthy fruits of repentance.*

He must increase, while I must decrease. —Jn 3:30

DEC. 4

REFLECTION. St. John the Baptist had the tragic fate to be the precursor of One Who was greater than he was. But this was also the reason for his greatness.

Christ is to increase and reign also in me. Therefore, I must struggle daily to eliminate all illegitimate self-esteem.

PRAYER. *Lord, make me humble so that You can give Yourself to me.*

DEC. 5

No one can see the reign of God unless he is begotten from above.
—Jn 3:3

REFLECTION. The Kingdom of God demands souls renewed in spirit. Therefore, we must undergo a total transformation of ourselves—not externally through a corporal rebirth, but internally through the redemptive work of God.

Only those who are truly open, without any reservation, to the Spirit of God become new persons in Christ.

PRAYER. *Come, Holy Spirit, and work in me the miracle of an inner transformation. Let me be moved only by You.*

DEC. 6

To you I lift up my soul, O Lord, my God. In you I trust. —Ps 25:1

REFLECTION. Every day that passes shows me clearly how much my soul is far from being redeemed and how slothful it still is.

This is why my main concern must be confident and constant prayer to the Redeemer. Only in Him is there Redemption.

PRAYER. *Lord, if You will, even today You can bring about in me a rebirth of soul. Help me to obtain this by Your grace.*

The day draws near. —Rom 13:12

DEC.
7

REFLECTION.   I must awake from my slumber. I must lead a life in Christ, with Christ, and for Christ.

Then there will be full daylight, the day of God, in my soul and I will have no fear on the day of Judgment.

PRAYER.   *Spirit of God, eliminate all darkness from my heart. Sanctify my thoughts, words, and actions, so that I may become a child of light.*

Rejoice, O highly favored daughter, the Lord is with you.
—Lk 1:28

DEC.
8

REFLECTION.   Not even the slightest sin nor any imperfection could touch the Virgin Mother of God. This was required by the dignity of her Divine Son.

Do I dwell on the fact that I too am a bearer of God? And do I try to have the most perfect purity of heart that this requires?

PRAYER.   *O Mary, conceived without sin, make my heart pure.*

177

DEC.
9

Let us put on the armor of light.
—Rom 13:13

REFLECTION. I must become a soul of light. For this I need the armor of light to be able to banish the powers of darkness.

Human forces are not enough. I need God's grace to walk in the light of day and dispel the darkness.

PRAYER. *Lord, be my protection and strength. Let me walk in the light of Your grace.*

DEC.
10

No one who waits for you shall be put to shame.
—Ps 25:3

REFLECTION. I must do all that is expected of me. Then I can confidently expect from my Father what will lead me to salvation.

God will even perform a miracle rather than deceive the soul of His child.

PRAYER. *Holy Spirit, give me faith according to the greatness of Your power. Come to my help according to the measure of my faith.*

Truth shall spring out of the earth, and justice shall look down from heaven.
—Ps 85:12

DEC. 11

REFLECTION. We are called to this: to bear fruit and to become saints in the Kingdom of God. Can I assume this important mission?

Nothing is lacking to God's blessing which is mine for the asking. In like manner, nothing must be lacking to my zeal and my collaboration.

PRAYER. *My Father, You expect great things from me. Help me with the blessings of Your grace, that I may accomplish these things according to Your will.*

The heavens and the earth will pass away, but my words will not pass.
—Lk 21:33

DEC. 12

REFLECTION. God always keeps His word, for He is eternal Truth. What about me?

Am I always truthful in everything I say? Am I always aware that every word of mine will one day be a witness for or against me before God's tribunal?

PRAYER. *Faithful God, let me always speak the truth so that I may answer to it without fear.*

DEC. 13

Are you "He who is to come" or do we look for another?

—Mt 11:3

REFLECTION. Why do I go around seeking help from everybody but God? God is always near me and He will never deceive or disappoint me.

He will fill me with His spiritual gifts: justice, peace, and joy in the Holy Spirit.

PRAYER. *Lord and Savior, You are within me by Your grace. Remain in me and make me always more spiritual through Your Holy Spirit.*

DEC. 14

Blest is the man who finds no stumbling block in me.

—Mt 11:6

REFLECTION. It is difficult to understand the ways of God which are so far above our own. Our ambitions are frequently of a worldly nature and because of them we are almost scandalized by Him.

It would be much better to examine our own selves so as to conform our ways to God's and be able better to serve Him and others with love and fidelity.

PRAYER. *Lord, You are eternal wisdom and patience. Give me light and strength, so that I may see and confess You in everything, even in things I do not understand.*

I am the servant of the Lord. Let it be done to me as you say.

—Lk 1:38

DEC. 15

REFLECTION. Everything that happens to me every day and every hour is a call from God. I must take care to answer Him with prompt dedication and a disposition open to sacrifice.

Then I will possess the secret of Mary, which is that of the Incarnation: God in me!

PRAYER. *Heavenly Father, let me be always prompt to obey You. I want to be Yours and to live in everything according to Your will.*

Rejoice in the Lord always!

—Phil 4:4

DEC. 16

REFLECTION. Joy is a Christian's duty. A joyful Christian honors his faith, while a sad one often turns others away from the Gospel.

Why shouldn't I rejoice? Is not Christ, my brother, stronger than sin, suffering, and death?

PRAYER. *Dear God, let me rejoice always in You. Help me to be a messenger of happiness to my brothers and sisters.*

DEC. 17

Dismiss all anxiety from your minds. Present your needs to God.
—Phil 4:6

REFLECTION. To prepare and provide are good things. However unrelieved anxiety serves only to paralyze us.

I want to place all my worries in the hands of the Father. He always provides for me.

PRAYER. *Heavenly Father, I give You thanks because Your love never ends. Grant me everything that I need for my soul and my body.*

DEC. 18

Everyone should see how unselfish you are. The Lord is near.
—Phil 4:5

REFLECTION. The Lord wants to come to us with mercy and love. I too should spread love to prepare the way for Him and become worthy of His love.

Do I seek to serve others so that the Lord will come to them through me?

PRAYER. *My Savior and Redeemer, let me radiate Your goodness to others. Help me to kindle the light of love and peace in all those I meet, so that I may prepare for Your coming.*

There is one among you whom you do not recognize. —Jn 1:26

DEC.
19

REFLECTION. Christ is in our churches, but He is also in every person. Am I convinced of this and do I show it in the way I act with others?

How terrible if one day I would hear the judgment: "I do not know you because you did not recognize Me in My brothers and sisters!"

PRAYER. *My Savior, do not let me forget that You are close to me. Help me always to see You in other people.*

How can this be? —Lk 1:34

DEC.
20

REFLECTION. Even if I do not see Him, my attitude to God must not change. His omnipotence, wisdom, and goodness are always the assurance of a good end.

This is why I want to place with confidence in His hands all the events of my life. Whatever God does is well done.

PRAYER. *Lord, lead me wherever You will. Without reservations I abandon myself to You.*

DEC. 21

Do not fear, Mary, You have found favor with God. —Lk 1:30

REFLECTION. The Lord has called me also and has accepted me in His love. He has filled me with all the richness of His grace.

Therefore, I must put away from me all anxieties and worries, doubts and scruples. God's omnipotence and love are infinite.

PRAYER. *Lord and Father, my trust in You is boundless. With Your hand You have taken me into Your loving care and You will guide me during life and in death.*

DEC. 22

Nothing is impossible with God. —Lk 1:37

REFLECTION. When God calls I do not need to ask Him any questions—just obey Him. I do not need to understand but to trust.

Nothing is impossible to Him. He helps me according to the measure of my trust.

PRAYER. *My Father, You are all-powerful. Turn my worries into trust, my depression into serenity, and my disquietude into security and peace.*

Say to those whose hearts are frightened: Be strong, fear not!
—Is 35:4

DEC.
23

REFLECTION. The Son of God comes as a child so that I may put away all anxiety and fear. How great is God's grace and kindness!

This should inspire in me a boundless confidence and an unceasing gratitude expressed in words and deeds.

PRAYER. *Most loving God, I give You thanks for the Incarnation of Your Son. Fear and anxiety must disappear in Your presence, because I know how much You love me.*

See, your king shall come to you.
—Zec 9:9

DEC.
24

REFLECTION. The beautiful Child in the manger is my brother. But He is also my God and my Divine King to Whom I owe worship, obedience, love, and fidelity until I die.

Is my life dedicated to serving this King without reservation and without deviation?

PRAYER. *Jesus, for You I live; Jesus, for You I die; Jesus, I want to be Yours in life and in death.*

DEC. 25

This day a Savior has been born.
—Lk 2:11

REFLECTION. Today we stand in awe at the tremendous event before us. The Son of God Himself comes as a beautiful Child lying in a manger! Now heaven and earth are united! God takes the hand of sinful human beings and raises them to His Divine life.

I want to go to Jesus Who is filled with joy. From His fullness I hope to receive grace upon grace.

PRAYER. *Dear Infant Jesus, let me be all Yours.*

DEC. 26

Glory to God in high heaven, peace on earth to those on whom his favor rests.
—Lk 2:14

REFLECTION. God's honor and glory is the final purpose of all Divine revelation. It is also the purpose of all human life.

When God is honored, all envy and argument disappear. There is peace even on earth.

PRAYER. *Lord, let my whole life be one continuous hymn of praise to You. May it give honor to You and bring joy and peace to human beings.*

He was manifested in the flesh.
—1 Tm 3:16

DEC. 27

REFLECTION.   The humble Child in the manger does not reveal to us the majesty and glory of God. But He does reveal something about God—His infinite love.

God's love is so great that He humbles Himself to the utmost in order to be near us in love.

PRAYER.   *Divine Child, I wish to love You as You have loved me.*

To his own he came, yet his own did not accept him.   —Jn 1:11

DEC. 28

REFLECTION.   Through creation and redemption I belong to the Savior. If I do not recognize His right of ownership, I will not be able to receive Him and will cut myself off from My Savior and Redeemer.

Only in Christ can I find my happiness in this world and for all eternity.

PRAYER.   *O my Savior and Redeemer, take full possession of my heart. It must become Your property and Your dwelling. Let me live in Your Divine Heart.*

DEC. 29

Any who did accept him he empowered to become children of God.
—Jn 1:12

REFLECTION. To be God's child means to be in holy conversation with the heavenly Father, to walk holding His hand, and to rest in His Heart for all eternity.

This is the greatest miracle that can be granted to a soul: to accept Christ and let Him reign in one's life. Who possesses my heart?

PRAYER. *My Lord and Savior, may everything I do and everything I possess be consecrated to You. Help me so that I may always behave as a child of God.*

DEC. 30

Walk while you still have light or darkness will come over you.
—Jn 12:35

REFLECTION. Without God everything is fearful darkness, but with God everything is light. My own way, no matter how dark the future may be, is totally bathed in this light.

I want to walk in it with courage and love because I know that my Savior is with me. In the new year I must also go toward the day of Christ.

PRAYER. *O Jesus, my guide, be near me and stay with me. Do not stray from my eternal destiny.*

Stay with us. It is nearly eve-
ning—the day is practically over.
—Lk 24:29

REFLECTION. This is a wonderful prayer to be said at the year's end. Without God life itself becomes impossible. With God, everything is sanctified and blessed—every step and every initiative.

In the year that is about to begin, I must let Christ be my Guide. Then my life will be one happy ascent to the Father—even if the way is strewn with thorns and bathed in blood.

PRAYER. *Lord, let everything be in Your hands—the beginning and the end.*